UNFINISHED BUSINESS

A Civil Rights Strategy for America's Third Century

Clint Bolick

PACIFIC RESEARCH INSTITUTE FOR PUBLIC POLICY
San Francisco, California

Cloth ISBN 0-936488-35-2
Paperback ISBN 0-936488-36-0

Library of Congress Catalog Card Number 90-7332

Printed in the United States of America.

Pacific Reseach Institue for Public Policy
177 Post Street
San Francisco, CA 94108
(415) 989-0833

Library of Congresss Cataloging-in-Publication Data

Bolick, Clint
Unfinished business: a civil rights strategy for America's third
century / by Clint Bolick.
    p.   cm.
  Includes bibliographical references.
  Includes index.
  ISBN 0-936488-35-2: $24.95. — ISBN 0-936488-36-0
  (pbk.): $12.95.
1. Civil rights—United States. I. Title
KF4749.555 1990
347.30285   90-7332
                                                CIP

For Mary

CONTENTS

Acknowledgements   vii

Foreword   ix
—*Charles Murray*

Introduction   1

Part I
Competing Visions of Civil Rights   11

Part II
Protecting Fundamental Individual Rights:
Dismantling Liberty's *Slaughter-House*   47

Part III
Topping *Plessy* v. *Ferguson:*
Individual Empowerment through Equality under Law   93

Part IV

Tactical Considerations and Concluding Observations   135

Appendix 1

**Ten Commandments for a Successful Public Interest
Litigation Strategy**   139

Appendix 2

Litigation Prototypes   145

Index   151

About the Author   159

ACKNOWLEDGEMENTS

This manuscript is a product of the Center for Applied Jurisprudence of the Pacific Research Institute for Public Policy in San Francisco. The Center's mission is to chart practical litigation strategies to advance the natural rights principles on which our nation was founded, specifically in the areas of property, First Amendment, and civil rights jurisprudence.

I was greatly aided in the daunting task of formulating such a litigation blueprint in the area of civil rights by the distinguished task force empaneled by the Center for that purpose. The task force consisted of many of the nation's foremost scholars and litigators in civil rights and related fields including Professor William B. Allen, Claremont-McKenna College; Professor Randy E. Barnett, Illinois Institute of Technology, Chicago-Kent College of Law; Charles Cooper, McGuire, Woods, Battle & Boothe; Professor Robert Detlefsen, California State University-San Bernardino; Professor Steven Eagle, George Mason University; Professor Edward Gaffney, Stanford University; Michael Greve,

Center for Individual Rights; Manuel Klausner, Kindel & Anderson; William H. (Chip) Mellor III, president of Pacific Research Institute; Professor Jeremy Rabkin, Cornell University; Professor Jennifer Roback, George Mason University; Professor Walter Berns, Georgetown University; Professor Nathan Glazer, Harvard University; Professor Leonard Liggio, Institute for Humane Studies; Jay Parker, Lincoln Institute; and Jeffrey Zuckerman, Curtis, Mallet-Prevost, Colt & Mosle. This manuscript reflects the insights and influence of all of these individuals, for which I am greatly indebted. However, I have neither sought nor received endorsements of the final product from any of these people; the ultimate conclusions and shortcomings of the manuscript are solely my own.

I greatly appreciate the research assistance provided by Ann Coulter, a law graduate of the University of Michigan who presently serves as a law clerk to Judge Pasco Bowman of the United States Court of Appeals for the Eighth Circuit; and Mary Chlopecki, a law student at George Mason University, who is also my collaborator in the forthcoming *Grass Roots Tyranny and the Limits of Federalism* (Cato Institute). I am grateful as well to the Institute for Humane Studies, which provided access to its fine library.

Primary credit, of course, belongs to the Pacific Research Institute and its president, Chip Mellor, for their vision and consistently first-rate guidance and assistance. To all those involved in this effort, I express my sincere gratitude and the hope that this manuscript reflects, in part, the sum of their substantial contributions.

FOREWORD

Unfinished Business is about the civil rights movement; it is written by a person whom most people would call a conservative; and it calls for sweeping reform to break the logjam that has choked black progress—all of which goes to show that political pigeonholes aren't what they used to be.

To liberals who have picked up *Unfinished Business*, you haven't made a mistake. There are no hidden agendas, no closet arguments for restoring the good old days when states were states and the federal government left them alone. To conservatives who have picked up *Unfinished Business*, don't expect comforting excuses and modest goals. Clint Bolick is a radical in the tradition of his hero, Thomas Paine. The reason the book comes as such a surprise is the discomfiting reality that conservatives have a history of being wrong about civil rights—not wrong in the policy positions conservatives have taken, necessarily, but wrong in failing to be part of the solution and thereby (yes, the Sixties radicals got it right, at least this one time) being part of the problem.

The right's detachment toward civil rights extended from the end of Reconstruction through the first half of the twentieth century, but it became most obvious during the epochal decade that began with the Montgomery bus boycott in 1955 and ended with the Voting Rights Act in 1965. Doubtless most conservatives, if asked, would have said that they favored equal rights before the law for everyone, but few of them said so loudly. Where was the passion? Where was the readiness to ride on the Freedom Buses? To go to jail? To proclaim enthusiastically that the essence of the American ideal is to treat people according to what they make of themselves, not the color of their skin? Whatever the reasons for the failure of the right to be in the forefront of this American drama, that failure had profound consequences for the evolution of civil rights in the post-1965 period.

The first of these consequences occurred during the debate over the Civil Rights Act of 1964. Because conservatives had borne none of the costs or suffering that led to that triumph, they were in no position to make the crucial argument that there is a big difference between prohibiting *governments* from discriminating according to race (which was imperative) and prohibiting *individuals* from so discriminating (which has much more complex implications). One must doubt whether the Civil Rights Act of 1964 could have been changed in any case—the combination of the moral power of the civil rights movement and the emotional aftermath of Kennedy's assassination as orchestrated by Lyndon Johnson was overwhelming. And many conservatives—Clint Bolick among them—support the Civil Rights Act of 1964 in its entirety, arguing that the monumental wrong it tried to right justified its modest restrictions on private behavior. But whatever the debate's outcome, this core tenet of Jeffersonian democracy should have been a legitimate part of the debate: Just as freedom of the press depends on a newspaper's right to print objectionable opinions, liberty itself depends ultimately on the principle that individuals acting privately, not forcing others to collaborate, may do things that are foolish and even morally objectionable. In 1964, the only people trying to make that point were Southerners fighting to protect practices that the nation could no longer stomach, and in the process the principle itself was reviled.

The second consequence of the right's detachment toward civil rights involves the assumption, first made legitimate by the implementation of the Civil Rights Act of 1964, that it is proper to legislate on behalf of a group of people if the cause is good, setting some American citizens apart from other Americans before the law. Conservatives, who had neglected efforts to enforce equality of individuals before the law for so long, were not in a position to mount the ethical and legal case against the subtle dangers of that doctrine. Those subtle dangers became apparent in 1965 when Lyndon Johnson embraced equal outcomes as the true test of effective civil rights measures. If blacks as a group did not exhibit the same outcomes, then it was proper to pass legislation that not only would permit but actually would require, with the force of civil and criminal penalties behind it, that people discriminate by race. Before long we had entered the era in which it was politically expedient to apply the same logic to any group that had enough political clout to claim special, discriminated-against status, and we began to weave the crazy quilt of group-based privileges and prohibitions that is still expanding.

Saddest, the white conservatives who had failed during the civil rights movement to affirm with passion and power that blacks must be treated equally before the law were not in a position to take a stand against the transformation from blacks-as-people-like-us to blacks-as-victims. At the apex of the civil rights movement in the summer of 1964, blacks had attained precisely that status in the white consciousness that was necessary for continued progress. The civil rights movement had made mainstream white America painfully aware of the injustices that had been done to blacks by whites, and yet blacks refrained from asking for anything more than equal treatment. The moral content of that combination was overpowering, and it gave blacks an appropriately lofty moral stature. The American system had violated its own ideals and made blacks victims of its failure. Blacks prevailed by forcing the system to cleanse itself. The stage was set for what should have been a period of racial conciliation and integration that would have been an example to the world.

Perhaps inevitably at such a point, when white guilt was at its most acute, some whites not only cried "mea culpa" for the sins of their race but decided to stop treating blacks as people like everyone else and instead to grant them moral exemption. In policy and intellectual circles, these voices came to dominate. Were black crime rates much higher than those of whites? It was the fault of unemployment and poverty and racism. Was the black illegitimacy rate several times that of whites and climbing steeply? In black culture, the extended family would compensate. Were young black men dropping out of the labor market? Unemployment was only reasonable if the alternative was a low-paying menial job. In rhetoric, legislation, regulatory reform, and court decisions, usually tacitly but often explicitly, the message went out: Blacks cannot be held to the same standards to which whites were ready to hold other whites. When conservatives tried to say that this new view of blacks was condescending and destructive, why should anyone believe that it was anything more than the same old curmudgeonly tune, "Let Them Fend for Themselves," with new lyrics?

Each of these three trends in the evolution of civil rights—toward regulation of private behavior, preferential legislation for groups, and double standards for whites and blacks—was latently poisonous. During the 1970s, the poison began to set it. Schemes for aggressive, court-ordered school busing infuriated white parents. Quota-based affirmative action plans for hiring new employees alienated blue-collar workers. White students in the nation's universities watched their black counterparts being admitted with lower test scores and special dispensations. By the 1980s, we had achieved the worst possible world, in which whites were resentful, a self-righteous civil rights rhetoric had lost its moral energy, and blacks themselves, especially low-income blacks, were losing ground. Meanwhile, conservatives too often accepted the political advantages of this situation without framing an affirmative vision of what the nation should be trying to accomplish.

Against this backdrop comes Clint Bolick, one of a small but growing band of new civil rights activists (in my view the only true idealists left in the civil rights movement). Too young to remember the events of the 1960s, Bolick remembers instead ideas of the 1780s, when a radical new view of man and his relationship to government led to the experiment called the United States. To him, the meaning of civil rights for blacks is uncomplicated and constitutes a moral imperative for action: People have the inalienable right to live out their lives free of interference so long as they engage in peaceful, voluntary, mutual transactions with others.

Fine words, one may respond, but what do they have to do with the price of bread, with getting a decent place to live, with fashioning a life for one's family in a ravaged inner city? Bolick identifies an answer in an aspect of liberty that was ignored during the mainstream civil rights movement, economic liberty. He then identifies a nuts-and-bolts legal strategy, strikingly reminiscent of the NAACP's implacably patient legal battle that led ultimately to *Brown* v. *Board of Education*, for expanding that liberty where it is needed most, in the poorest and most isolated of the nation's communities. In making this case, Bolick is indignant, passionate, compassionate, and an unabashed activist—all the things that conservatives should have been a quarter-century ago.

Most of Clint Bolick's life these days is spent in the courtroom. But I doubt that legal victories alone will win this fight, any more than legal victories alone moved the nation in the decade after Rosie Parks refused to sit at the back of a Montgomery bus. It is essential as well to make the intellectual and moral case that Bolick's way is right, which is why this small book is so important.

Charles Murray

Introduction

FRAMEWORK FOR A CIVIL RIGHTS LITIGATION STRATEGY

I have spent much of the past two years working in the courts for a new direction for civil rights. I attempt in this manuscript first to sketch briefly why such a change of direction is necessary and then in greater detail to outline a litigation strategy to facilitate that new course. If I am correct in my premise that America's moral claim is staked in its doctrinal commitment to civil rights, then our nation's future rests in large measure in the choices we make over the next several years with respect to a civil rights strategy.

This manuscript builds in significant measure from my previous book, *Changing Course: Civil Rights at the Crossroads*,[1] which first introduced the policy blueprint on which I expand here. I commenced each of that book's chapters with quotations of Thomas Paine, whose keen insights into the nature and importance of civil rights are as relevant to the quest for civil rights today as they were two centuries ago. In preparing this manuscript, I drew special inspiration from two of Paine's admonitions to his fellow revolutionaries, both of which captured the heady spirit of the age—a spirit we need badly to rekindle in America today. Said Paine,

> We must return to first principles . . . and *think*, as if we were the first men that thought.[2]

What Paine meant by "first principles" was that immutable body of law derived from the nature of people as rational beings—the law of nature that has from the beginning of human beings guided and nurtured their progress and development. Paine urged his compatriots to apply the principles of natural law to the changing circumstances attending societal evolution; by doing so, he correctly argued, they could throw off the yoke of monarchial oppression and reassert their nature as free and sovereign individuals.

Paine also boldly declared that "We have the power to begin the world over again."[3] The "power" Paine referred to, of course, was not the coercive apparatus of the state, but rather the power of the ideas of liberty. Martin Luther King, Jr., recognized this awesome power two hundred years later when—to define the moral framework for the civil rights revolution of his own era—he quoted Paine and invoked the "first principles" embodied in our nation's Declaration of Independence.

These quotations from Paine speak pointedly to the theme of *Changing Course*, and they inform this work as well. In *Changing Course*, I argued that civil rights are those fundamental rights that we all share equally as Americans—specifically, the natural rights of life, liberty, and the pursuit of happiness, protected in equal measure for all by the basic law of the land. This commitment was expressed in our nation's charter, the Declaration of Independence, which declared that "all men are created equal," and are "endowed by their Creator with certain unalienable Rights," among which are "Life, Liberty and the pursuit of Happiness." Thus did the Declaration of Independence establish the two components of the civil rights "equation": fundamental individual rights and equality under law.

This understanding of civil rights as natural rights enshrined in civil law was shared by every great advocate of civil rights, from Paine to Frederick Douglass to William Lloyd Garrison to Martin Luther King, Jr. That traditional vision of civil rights fueled all the movement's greatest triumphs, from the revolution against the crown, to the abolition of slavery, to the great civil rights enactments following the Civil War, to the Civil Rights Act of 1964 and its progeny.

Yet in many respects, it seems that of late the quest for civil rights has lost its momentum. Indeed, the very meaning of civil rights, so well understood by its great proponents during America's first two centuries, seems hopelessly confused today. The civil rights movement, which served for so long as our nation's conscience, has lost sight of its mission and has drifted recklessly off course for a generation.

Were we to seek Paine's sage counsel today, he would advise us, as Martin Luther King did a quarter century ago, to return again to first principles and to apply those principles to our present dilemmas. Those principles, he would assure us, would indeed empower us to change the world—to make good, at long last, on America's promise of civil rights for all its people. What follows here is precisely such an attempt at "applied principles": an examination of the natural law principles of civil rights accompanied by a practical framework from which to apply those principles to contemporary civil rights issues.

This framework will require an approach markedly different from that advocated by the contemporary civil rights establishment. During the past 25 years, that establishment has abandoned the principles that produced the civil rights movement's greatest victories.[4] It has grown complacent, elitist, patronizing, and increasingly detached from the needs of its claimed constituency, demanding as a civil rights litmus test fidelity to a failed agenda of racial quotas, busing, and set-asides.[5]

Yet despite this vacuum of leadership, those who have questioned the revised civil rights agenda have failed to adequately capture the terms of the debate. I do not mean to diminish in any way the tremendous accomplishments of those who have engaged courageously in this battle, but I merely assert that a strategy that consists mainly of resisting the civil rights establishment's agenda is by nature a losing strategy, for a variety of reasons. First, a reactive posture allows the other side to define civil rights issues in terms of its own agenda and to claim the moral high ground. Those who set the agenda enjoy an "enormous advantage," argues Nathan Glazer, since they "are seen as moral, and a moral advantage in politics, being on the side of right, is worth a good deal."[6] As a result, any time a victory is scored for one of the seminal tenets of civil rights that falls outside the scope of the civil rights establishment's agenda, such as racial neutrality, that triumph is somehow perceived widely as a "defeat" for civil rights.

Moreover, a purely defensive approach overlooks the vast amount of unfinished business we have in securing fundamental individual rights for all Americans. Millions of individuals in our society are today more isolated from basic opportunities by artificial and arbitrary barriers than ever before; until those barriers are eradicated, the quest for civil rights is not complete. We cannot revive a broad moral consensus on civil rights with a strategy that concerns itself primarily with challenges to "reverse" discrimination but speaks not at all to the circumstances of those who have been most severely victimized by civil rights deprivations. Abstract invocations of a "color-blind society" ring hollow unless accompanied by a demonstrated commitment to make good on the promise of civil rights for all Americans.

Stuart Butler, director of domestic policy studies at the Heritage Foundation, recently remarked that "[c]onfidence is not engendered [among black Americans] by conservative attorneys chasing firetrucks to see if any members of the Teamsters Union are upset about affirmative action."[7] This does not mean that advocates of the traditional civil rights vision should not stand firmly against discrimination whether visited on whites or blacks, but rather that reverse discrimination claims ought not form the centerpiece of a civil rights strategy. Butler urges instead an emphasis on the most disadvantaged in our society through practical strategies designed to foster individual empowerment. In particular, Butler urges policy reforms such as urban enterprise zones, and tenant management and ownership of public housing.[8] Likewise, I have recently profiled a number of innovative, non-coercive, highly workable "affirmative action" strategies that can bridge the skills, information, and culture gaps that separate economically disadvantaged individuals from job opportunities.[9] Such reforms can do much to help those outside the economic mainstream break the cycle of dependency and despair, and earn their share of the American Dream.

Already, the pioneers of this empowerment strategy are starting to make their ideas a reality. Robert Woodson of the National Center for Neighborhood Enterprise, Housing and Urban Development Secretary Jack Kemp, Education Secretary Lauro Cavazos, and Representative Steve Bartlett (R-TX), chairman of an empowerment caucus in the House of Representatives, are championing a variety of empowerment initiatives ranging from urban homesteading to education vouchers.

One advantage of this empowerment strategy is that it by definition *expands* opportunities, as opposed to contemporary civil rights policies that merely redistribute rights. This latter approach is a zero-sum game: every beneficiary's gain is someone else's loss. We are today witnessing the sad consequences of that agenda: on one hand, it has done nothing to solve the problems of the predominantly black underclass; on the other hand, it has fueled the resurgence of racial polarization. Our nation cannot fulfill its promise until all Americans perceive a direct and equal stake in civil rights.

Empowerment is also a winning strategy because it proposes real solutions to the problems of real people, the very people whom the civil rights policies of the past were supposed to help. The empowerment strategy goes to the core of the traditional American vision of civil rights because it focuses on giving people the power to control their own destinies.

In a very real sense, empowerment represents the ultimate accomplishment of civil rights. The quest for civil rights in America can be divided into three distinct phases, each defined in terms of its overriding objective. The first phase, corresponding roughly with the nation's first century, was concerned with the abolition of slavery. The second phase, commencing with the Fourteenth Amendment and culminating in *Brown* v. *Board of Education*[10] and the Civil Rights Act of 1964, was focused largely on achieving equal rights—a task that is not yet fully complete. In addition to more effectively securing equal rights, the civil rights movement in America's third century can complete its mission by achieving the goal of individual empowerment.

A vigorous and effective litigation strategy is essential to this effort. Civil rights are by definition individual rights and are most frequently asserted against the government. In our constitutional scheme, the judiciary is entrusted with the ultimate responsibility of safeguarding fundamental individual rights.[11] Though the courts have engaged in much mischief in recent years by creating civil rights entitlements from thin air, it is an equally obnoxious and debilitating form of judicial activism for the courts to fail to fully implement intended constitutional protections. Advocates of the traditional civil rights vision ought to help steer the courts in a principled direction, away from judicial activism and toward a more vigorous protection of fundamental individual rights.

Previous civil rights advocates have recognized the necessity of judicial action, which dates back at least as far as 1849 when Charles Sumner challenged segregated public education in the courts.[12] In 1905, recognizing that legislative efforts to achieve basic civil rights protections were futile, a group of black intellectuals met at Niagara Falls to chart a methodical, practical, and principled long-range litigation strategy to achieve equality under law.[13] That strategy, implemented by the National Association for the Advancement of Colored People (NAACP) and its allies, led eventually to *Brown* v. *Board of Education* and the collapse of the "separate but equal" doctrine. That triumph demonstrated how much can be accomplished through passion, persistence, effective lawyering, and steadfast adherence to basic principles.

As with the NAACP's strategy leading up to *Brown*, the Fourteenth Amendment necessarily provides the focus for a positive strategy of contemporary civil rights litigation that will achieve equality under law plus fundamental individual rights. As I will discuss subsequently, the Fourteenth Amendment embodies, and was intended to fulfill, the civil rights vision I have described here. The Fourteenth Amendment provides a protection for individual liberty, both through a positive grant of natural rights to individuals in the "privileges or immunities" clause, and through restraints on government power in the equal protection and due process clauses.

These constitutional provisions are not mere philosophical abstractions. Every time government compromises these principles, it reduces individual autonomy in equal measure. Whether the departure from principle takes the form of a quota that keeps a young Asian student out of a state university or a government regulation that keeps an unemployed black man from starting his own business, the real-world consequences are devastating.

The litigation strategy outlined in the following pages is designed to implement fully the intended protections of individual liberty in the Fourteenth Amendment and related constitutional provisions. This strategy emphasizes the privileges or immunities clause and the equal protection clause, for a variety of reasons. First, these two clauses correlate with the two primary components of civil rights: fundamental individual rights and equality under law. Second, whereas the due process clause speaks principally to the requirements the government must meet before it infringes on the fundamental rights of life, liberty, and property, both the privileges or immunities clause and the equal protection clause create substantive barriers to the exercise of government power. In essence, if properly applied, these clauses create zones of individual autonomy that are inviolable. Finally, the greatest judicial departures from the principles embodied in the Fourteenth Amendment have taken place in the context of the privileges or immunities and equal protection clauses.

Specifically, two Supreme Court decisions that remain on the books severely compromise the values protected by the Fourteenth Amendment. The *Slaughter-House Cases* (1873)[14] virtually read the privileges or immunities clause out of the Constitution, leaving economic liberty and other important individual rights essentially unprotected. Similarly, *Plessy* v. *Ferguson* (1896)[15] largely negated the constitutional guarantee of equal protection of the laws. Though *Plessy* has been significantly limited by recent cases, its pernicious doctrine continues to influence contemporary jurisprudence. Toppling these two pillars of oppression is the overarching challenge in a litigation strategy reinvigorated by the first principles of civil rights.

Since May 1988, I have attempted to craft precisely such a litigation program as director of the Landmark Legal Foundation Center for Civil Rights. Each of the Center's cases is directed toward chipping away at *Slaughter-House* or *Plessy*. In the area of economic liberty, we are prosecuting cases in which the dreams and aspirations of individuals outside the economic mainstream are thwarted by excessive and arbitrary government regulations. In the area of equality under law, we are focusing on cases that illustrate the perverse consequences that inevitably flow from departures from that principle, specifically instances of race-consciousness that have ultimately harmed the intended beneficiaries of such policies. I shall draw upon several of these cases to illustrate my proposed long-range legal strategy.

This litigation strategy is by no means exhaustive. Rather, it constitutes a general outline and direction by which to advance traditional civil rights principles in the judicial arena. No shortage of creative minds exists to further refine and develop the ideas presented here and to pursue many other possible legal and political strategies in support of individual empowerment.

This strategy does, however, reflect a conscious decision to enter the fray and to join the debate over civil rights. I am mindful that some who would support the policy goals advocated here would refrain from doing so in the context of civil rights. The concept of civil rights is hopelessly lost, the argument goes; it is too late to reclaim it. I hope that view is incorrect. I believe we have already damaged the cause of civil rights too much by our absence from the debate. If the advocates of liberty are not the champions of civil rights, then I contend there are today no champions of civil rights. The mantle of civil rights is too important to lose by further abdication.

As someone who was only a youngster in the 1960s, I often wonder what it was like for those who were involved when the civil rights struggle was at its apex. There must have existed such a tremendous sense of energy, of mission, of dedication, of passion, of destiny.

That spirit, that excitement, is so tragically missing today. Are we so cynical that we cannot reclaim it?

I am, quite obviously, a dissenter from the prevailing contemporary civil rights orthodoxy. Simply stated, I cannot imagine this nation, let alone any sizable portion of it, summoning any great enthusiasm for a civil rights agenda grounded in reparations, unequal treatment, and dependency on the state. Conversely, I can quite vividly imagine the development of a spirited national consensus in favor of equal rights and individual empowerment.

I watch as the NAACP continues its insistence on failed policies, losing members by the thousands as its doctrinaire agenda grows more and more irrelevant to the needs of today's blacks.[16] I watch as millions of Americans within the "underclass" lose hope and dignity by the day. I wonder if perhaps a rediscovery of "first principles" might help to restore momentum to a civil rights movement that has drifted dangerously off course for a generation. By turning away from an agenda that divides us in favor of one that emphasizes the values and principles that unite us as Americans, perhaps we can finally attain the dream of which Martin Luther King, Jr., so eloquently spoke.

The accomplishment of civil rights, of course, will provide no panacea. It will not automatically end poverty, or unfairness, or racial prejudice. But it will ensure something that no amount of social engineering by government can possibly achieve: it will guarantee individuals the right to control their own destinies, which is the essence of civil rights. As columnist William Raspberry has remarked, "Enforcement of civil rights can ensure us only a place in the starting gate. What is required for victory is that we run like hell."[17]

As we head into the 1990s, much unfinished business remains in the quest for civil rights. Once again, Tom Paine's words are instructive: "Tyranny, like hell, is not easily conquered; yet we have this consolation with us, the harder the conflict, the more glorious the triumph."[18]

ENDNOTES

1.   Clint Bolick, *Changing Course: Civil Rights at the Crossroads* (New Brunswick, N.J.: Transaction Books, 1988).

2.   Harry Hayden Clark, ed., *Thomas Paine and the Rights of Man* (New York: Charles Scribner's Sons, 1971), p. xiv [emphasis in original].

3.   Quoted in Martin Luther King, Jr., *Where Do We Go from Here: Chaos or Community?* (New York: Harper and Row, Publishers, 1967), p. 70.

4.   For a superb analysis of this tragic evolution, see Morris Abram, "Affirmative Action: Fair Shakers and Social Engineers," 99 *Harv. L. Rev.* 1315 (1986).

5.   See generally Clint Bolick, *In Whose Name? The Civil Rights Establishment Today* (Washington: Capital Research Center, 1988).

6.   Nathan Glazer, *Affirmative Discrimination: Ethnic Inequality and Public Policy* (New York: Basic Books, 1975), p. 210.

7.   Stuart Butler, "Razing the Liberal Plantation," *National Review*, 10 November 1989, p. 28.

8.   *Id.*, p. 29.

9.   Clint Bolick and Susan Nestleroth, *Workforce 2000: Creative Affirmative Action Strategies for a Changing Workforce* (Washington: U.S. Department of Labor, 1988). See also Kevin Hopkins, Susan Nestleroth, and Clint Bolick, *Help Wanted: How Companies Can Survive and Thrive in the Coming Worker Shortage* (New York: McGraw-Hill, 1990).

10.   *Brown* v. *Board of Education of Topeka*, 347 U.S. 483 (1954).

11.   I argue in favor of the appropriateness and necessity of judicial action to protect civil rights in *Changing Course*, chap. 7.

12.   Bolick, *Changing Course*, p. 19.

13.   See Albert P. Blaustein and Robert L. Zangrando, eds., *Civil Rights and the American Negro* (New York: Trident Press, 1968), pp. 324-338.

14.   *Slaughter-House Cases*, 83 U.S. 36 (1872).

15.   *Plessy* v. *Ferguson*, 163 U.S. 537 (1896).

16.   For a revealing discussion of the growing schism in policy views between the civil rights leadership elite and its purported constituency, see Linda S. Lichter, "Who Speaks for Black America?" *Public Opinion* (August/September 1985): 42.

17.   William Raspberry, "The Civil Rights Movement Is Over," *Washington Post*, 25 February 1987, p. A23.

18.   Thomas Paine, *The American Crisis*, no. 1 (1776).

Part I

COMPETING VISIONS OF CIVIL RIGHTS

He's made us all a little bit freer.
> —Peter Jennings, World News Tonight,
> *speaking about Ego Brown, the*
> *successful plaintiff in* Brown v. Barry[1]

[It] really reflect[s] the nineteenth century, not the future.
> —Barry Goldstein, NAACP
> *Legal Defense and Educational Fund,*
> *speaking about the same case*[2]

Ego Brown never fancied himself a crusader, and surely he never pictured himself at the forefront of a burgeoning debate over the future direction of civil rights in America. But he is both.

On top of that, he's a darned good shoeshine artist.

Ego Brown had the courage and determination to make a federal case about shoeshining, or more specifically, about the enforcement of an 84-year-old law that prevented him from shining shoes on the streets of the nation's capital. His lawsuit against Mayor Marion Barry and the District of Columbia government was the opening salvo in the battle to make "economic liberty" the civil rights issue of the 1990s.[3]

It all started with an idea Ego Brown had one day as he stared out the window in the office he occupied as a voucher examiner for the Navy. He yearned for a business of his own, where he could be his own boss and reap his own profits.

Over time, Ego Brown discovered a potentially lucrative niche in the thousands of scuffed shoes pounding the pavement of Wash-

ington's downtown streets. As a youngster, Brown shined shoes for
pocket money. But then he noticed it was nearly impossible to find
a convenient shoeshine in the District.

Brown quit his government job and started shining shoes at a
barber shop near Howard University. Before long, he had
perfected his technique and was ready to "spread the shine." Clad
in his trademark tuxedo, Brown used his flamboyant personality
to lure customers to his outdoor stand. His long-range goal was to
one day operate stands on street corners throughout the city and
beyond.

Business went so well that Brown soon opened additional
stands. He staffed them with enterprising homeless individuals, to
whom Brown provided a second chance at life in the form of a
daily shower, a set of clothes, and training in the Ego shoeshine
method. "I used to see these people begging for money, and I'd dig
into my pockets to help them," he told me. "But one day, I realized
I could help them more by giving them an opportunity, a chance
to lift themselves by their own bootstraps." Brown's efforts to aid
the poor through bootstraps capitalism were so successful that a
District of Columbia social worker started referring promising
candidates to him from the ranks of the homeless.

But Ego Brown's dream soon disintegrated into a nightmare.
The police shut down his stands, citing a 1905 law that forbade
shoeshine stands on public streets. That law was one of many
passed during the Jim Crow era to prevent blacks from attaining
economic self-sufficiency through their own businesses. Despite
the law's sordid origins, and despite the abundance of other ven-
dors on the District's streets selling everything from hot dogs to
photo opportunities with cardboard Ronald Reagans, the government chose to enforce the law and thereby destroy Ego Brown's
enterprise.[4] During the next three years of trying to make a living
shining shoes in privately owned buildings, Brown was barely a
step away from the welfare rolls, his seemingly irrepressible spirit
nearly broken.

Yet remarkably, no one from the civil rights establishment rose to
Brown's defense. When my own organization filed a lawsuit,
establishment civil rights groups either were silent or hostile. An
attorney from the Lawyer's Committee for Civil Rights appeared

on television to defend the District's "police power" to regulate shoeshines for the public good. An NAACP Legal Defense Fund lawyer dismissed the lawsuit as a relic of the 19th century. An activist lawyer from the Equal Employment Opportunity Commission declared that shining shoes was not a dignified job, that Ego Brown would have more dignity on welfare. Ego Brown's struggle for justice would have to proceed without the help of the very groups that claim to speak on his behalf in matters of civil rights.

Meanwhile, half a continent away in Kansas City, the parents of Mark Anthony Nevels, a black youngster coming of school age, were preparing to enroll him in kindergarten. Fortunately for the Nevels family, the Weeks Elementary School just across the street had recently been converted to a high-quality "magnet" school, and there was plenty of space.

Plenty of space, that is, except for blacks.

Under the terms of a court-imposed desegregation order, the new magnet schools in Kansas City were required to conform to a rigid racial quota, allowing admission to three black students for every two whites who chose to attend. If whites elected not to attend, blacks were refused admission. The school district tried mightily to attract white students from the suburbs without much success. But rather than allowing black youngsters to take the empty seats, the school district chose to leave the seats unfilled.

In the case of Weeks Elementary School, there was room for 122 kindergarten students. But only four white children enrolled, and thus only six black children could be admitted. As a result, 112 seats were held empty, despite a waiting list of 86 black youngsters including little Mark Anthony Nevels. Mark would be bused past his neighborhood school to an inferior school, solely on account of his skin color.[5]

The magnet school's racial quota initially was vigorously defended by the establishment's civil rights lawyer representing the plaintiff class in the desegregation case. After all, he insisted, the goal of school desegregation was racial balance; any incidental quality educational opportunities that might result were merely a bonus. Eventually, he altered his view and requested a modification of the quota, but only after months of intense criticism from black community groups.

These cases present some curious spectacles. In the first, a self-professed civil rights lawyer took to the airwaves to justify the modern-day enforcement of a Jim Crow law. In the second, another civil rights lawyer defended a policy that forced black youngsters to travel past their neighborhood schools solely on account of their skin color. This latter spectacle is especially remarkable considering that the entire desegregation era commenced 35 years ago in *Brown* v. *Board of Education* with the Supreme Court striking down a policy that bused black students past their neighborhood schools solely because of skin color. Have we traveled so far only to end up in precisely the place we started?

CIVIL RIGHTS AT THE CROSSROADS

The widely divergent reactions to these two cases by people who describe themselves as civil rights advocates illustrate vividly the emergence, for the first time in American history, of two distinct and irreconcilable visions of civil rights. That those who would claim the mantle of civil rights would find themselves anywhere other than marching shoulder to shoulder with Ego Brown and Mark Anthony Nevels suggests that the civil rights movement has somewhere taken a wrong turn.

The quest for civil rights is in crisis. There exists today probably less consensus on the meaning of civil rights—what they are and to whom they belong—than at any time in our nation's history. This crisis of identity threatens to arrest, if not reverse, the painful yet steady progress we have made toward achieving civil rights for all Americans during the past 200 years.

In the contemporary lexicon, civil rights is a muddled term. In common usage, its content ranges from concrete, to amorphous, to empty. Often the term is used not as a freestanding concept that conveys clear substantive meaning, but rather as an adjective—civil rights leader, civil rights violation, civil rights legislation—in an effort to confer upon its object the moral imprimatur that attends an intrinsically righteous cause. That the invocation of this term can so powerfully stake a claim to the moral high ground is testimony to its noble lineage; that the same term is so confused and misunderstood suggests we have lost sight of its origins.

This phenomenon is not accidental. Many of those who today are most often identified as civil rights leaders embrace an ideology that is alien to the traditional American civil rights vision. That ideology has required such advocates to reject the principles underlying that traditional vision and to replace it with a very different conception of civil rights, giving the meaning of civil rights its present qualities of uncertainty and schizophrenia.

This abandonment of the traditional principles of civil rights has resulted in far more than confusion. By substituting the goal of equal opportunity with forced equality of result, the steady progress our nation was making in the 1950s and 1960s toward securing real opportunities for the most disadvantaged Americans has slowed to a virtual standstill. By substituting individual rights with group entitlements, the nation's consensus on civil rights has deteriorated, with support for civil rights made contingent upon one's vantage point. By any standard, the record of this revisionist agenda of civil rights pales starkly in comparison to the achievements secured through two centuries of fidelity to the original principles of civil rights.

What follows is an examination of the competing visions of civil rights and a comparison of their respective records in accomplishing those rights. I believe the record plainly shows that we can escape our present quagmire only by returning to the first principles of civil rights. From that foundation we can chart a coherent and effective strategy to vindicate those principles.

THE ORIGINAL CIVIL RIGHTS VISION

For two centuries Americans shared a common understanding of civil rights as natural rights—life, liberty, and property—enshrined in civil law. That view does not mean that everyone endorsed such rights, that everyone agreed on the boundaries of those rights, nor, by any means, that the rights were consistently honored. But in terms of the rights' basic meaning—and of their central position in the American system of government—a remarkable degree of consensus existed for nearly 200 years following the nation's founding. Certainly, all the great advocates of this vision, from Thomas Paine and Thomas Jefferson to Martin Luther King, shared that basic understanding. Indeed, in a very real sense America has fought at least three wars to defend and pre-serve that precious consensus: the American Revolution, to establish the civil rights of the colonists; the Civil War, to extend those rights to all Americans; and World War II, to protect those rights against totalitarianism.

This traditional vision of civil rights is grounded in a commit-ment to individual self-determination, and it recognizes that any attempt to use the state's power to go beyond that point will ulti-mately detract from the underlying goal of individual sovereignty. As Morris Abram explains, advocates of the traditional civil rights vision believe that "removing all barriers to the exercise of civil and political rights and to an individual's ability to participate in the free market system is the best possible way to promote justice." These objectives, Abram argues, "constitute the limits of what the *law* in the American system can do, *if that system is to remain free.*"[6]

This traditional civil rights vision is firmly grounded in the concept of natural law; yet it is for the most part a distinctively American term and relatively new to the popular vocabulary. Indeed, as Robert Detlefsen notes, the term "civil rights" does not appear in the Constitution, Bill of Rights, or Declaration of Inde-pendence. In fact, the term was "rarely used in American political discourse until after the Civil War."[7]

Nonetheless, the concept traces its origins to the early natural law theorists as they began to articulate various distinctions among types of rights: inalienable rights versus alienable rights, rights conferred on people by nature versus rights bestowed by government.

In his history of the theory of natural law, Otto Gierke traced these distinctions among types of rights to the philosophers Althusius and Grotius.[8] The significance of such distinctions grew, however, as later philosophers of natural law attempted to refute the arguments of Hobbes, Spinoza, and Rousseau, all of whom believed that individuals surrender some or all of their rights to the community when they leave the state of nature.[9] In response, Gierke explains, natural rights theorists argued that "the indi-vidual surrendered *only a part of his original rights* into the stock of society," a view leading to the corollary that "certain of the rights of the individual were inalienable and intransferable." In this way, Gierke observes,

> a distinction came to be drawn between inherent and acquired rights. Acquired rights, it was argued, were subject to the system of positive law, which depended for its existence on the State; but inherent rights were based on the pre-social Law of Nature, and since that law was still valid to protect them, they were immune from any invasion by legislative action.[10]

This "distinction between 'civil' and 'natural' rights," as Gierke described it,* was subsequently further "developed by Locke and the political economists in the interest of economic liberty."[11] For Locke, the only moral constraint on a human being's liberty was the "law of nature": "no one ought to harm another in his life, liberty, or possessions."[12] People organized governments in conformity with the law of nature by the terms of a "social compact," Locke explained, in order to more effectively secure maximum liberty. Since governments were formed to protect natural rights, they could not have authority to violate such rights.

These concepts were incorporated into the English common law as reflected in the writings of Sir William Blackstone and Chancellor James Kent.[13] Blackstone believed that individuals possessed three absolute rights: "the right of personal security, the right of personal liberty, and the right of private property."[14] In his *Commentaries*, Blackstone declared that "the principal aim of society is to protect individuals in the enjoyment of those absolute rights, which were vested in them by the immutable laws of nature." Hence, Blackstone reasoned, "the first and primary end of human laws is to maintain and regulate these *absolute* rights of individuals."[15]

These absolute rights, Blackstone observed, "are usually summed up in one general appellation, and denominated the natural liberty of mankind. This natural liberty consists properly

---

* Over time, as discussed later in this section, this distinction was recast in terms of "civil" versus "political" rights, with civil rights thereafter defined as natural rights that are retained after people enter society and political rights defined as those conferred by government. Confusion arises today when the term civil rights is used as a substitute for political rights, such as the right to vote or attend school.

in a power of acting as one thinks fit, without any restraint or control, unless by the law of nature."[16] Accordingly, such rights do not depend on a positive declaration by government but are instead included within the "*residuum* of natural liberty"[17]—a concept later embodied in the Ninth Amendment to the U.S. Constitution.

Like the earlier philosophers of natural law, Blackstone believed that humans surrendered only a small part of their natural liberty upon entering society, in return securing for themselves what Blackstone called "civil liberty," which he defined as "no other than natural liberty so far restrained by human laws (and no farther) as is necessary and expedient for the general advantage of the publick."[18] For Blackstone, then, "that constitution or frame of government, that system of laws, is alone calculated to maintain civil liberty, which leaves the subject entire master of his own conduct, except in those points wherein the public good requires some direction or restraint."[19]

The natural rights philosophers thus made a number of important contributions to what would later develop as the American civil rights vision. Perhaps most significantly, they recognized a realm of absolute individual autonomy in the form of the "inalienable" rights of life, liberty, and property. By such rights, they did not mean unqualified liberty or the ownership of particular property. Indeed, individuals can freely exchange a portion of their liberty or property for other values. Rather, what is inalienable is the basic liberty that is essential to an individual's ability to pursue happiness, as well as the related right to acquire and hold property. This inviolable realm of individual autonomy, consisting of the power to control one's own destiny, is the element common to all civil rights struggles, from the crusade against slavery to Ego Brown's battle for the right to earn a living.

How a particular individual exercises these rights is subject to qualification by government if that conduct affects the rights of others. But the underlying rights themselves, essential to the individual's persona, are not subject to compromise, regardless of the breadth of the majority's will. With respect to these fundamental rights, then, the "minority of one" is transformed into a majority of one.

Civil rights—the rights individuals retain when they leave a state of nature and form civil societies—consist of all the pre-existing natural rights save one: the right to judge one's own actions. The principal benefit of government is that it substitutes an objective system of justice for the subjectivity that existed in the state of nature. Beyond this minor sacrifice, which ultimately accrues to the benefit of every member of civil society, individuals do not relinquish any of their fundamental rights, which remain inalienable.

These principles of natural rights, particularly the natural law concept of civil rights, were firmly embraced by the founders of the American republic and by the system of government they created. More than any other philosopher of the period, Thomas Paine formulated a coherent rights framework in the Locke-Blackstone tradition and more fully developed the distinct concept of "civil rights" that would provide the philosophical foundation for the American civil rights vision.

That Paine had a profound impact on the philosophical evolution of the new nation is beyond question. John Adams, one of Paine's principal antagonists, remarked in 1805 that "I know not whether any man in the world has had more influence on its inhabitants or affairs for the last thirty years than Paine."[20] Eric Foner states that Paine's *Common Sense* "reached literally hundreds of thousands of readers in the single year 1776"; Foner declares that the tract was "central to the explosion of political argument beyond the confines of a narrow, educated elite to 'all ranks' of Americans."[21]

Paine understood "civil rights" as the motivation for and consequence of people leaving a state of nature and entering society— that is, to gain security for their natural rights. For Paine, a civil right was "a natural right exchanged" upon entering society.[22] Paine explained,

Man did not enter society to become *worse* than he was before, nor to have less rights than he had before, but to have those rights better secured. His natural rights are the foundation of all of his civil rights. . . . Natural rights are those which always appertain to man in right of his existence . . . Civil rights are those which appertain to man in right of his being a member of society. Every civil right has for its foundation some natural right pre-existing in the individual, but to which his individual power is not, in all cases, sufficiently competent.[23]

Paine agreed with Locke and Blackstone that the primary purpose of government is to protect fundamental rights, and that those rights are inviolable, regardless of the degree of majoritarian will. If the majority could negate or compromise an individual's fundamental rights, such rights were in no meaningful sense inalienable; likewise, a government devised to protect such rights would surrender its moral legitimacy if it facilitated invasions of those rights. Thus, Paine declared, "[T]he power produced by the aggregate of natural rights, imperfect in power in the individual, cannot be applied to invade the natural rights which are retained in the individual."[24]

The inviolability of the fundamental individual rights of life, liberty, and property thus formed the cornerstone of the American civil rights vision. Paine understood, however, that something more was needed to finish the equation. Paine recognized that individual rights were vulnerable to majoritarian tyranny unless those rights were protected for all in equal measure. Paine emphasized that "[w]henever I use the words *freedom* or *rights*, I desire to mean a perfect equality of them. . . . It is this broad base, this universal foundation, that gives security to all and every part of society."[25] As Paine explained,

> In a state of nature, all men are equal in rights but they are not equal in power; the weak cannot protect themselves against the strong. This being the case, the institution of civil society is for the purpose of making an equalization of powers that shall be parallel to, and a guarantee of, the equality of rights. The laws of a country, when properly constructed, apply to this purpose.[26]

Paine recognized that equality of rights would not necessarily lead to equality in outcome. "That property will ever be unequal is certain," he remarked. "Industry, superiority of talents, dexterity of management, extreme frugality, fortunate opportunities, or the opposite, or the means of those things, will ever produce that effect."[27] Rather, for Paine, the moral virtue of absolute equality of rights was that it rendered any departure from the principle "a question of force, and not of right."[28]

Paine bolstered the moral case for equality of rights by stressing the reciprocal nature of the protection. Paine observed, for instance, that "the rich have no more right to exclude the poor from the right of voting, or of electing and being elected, than the poor have a right to exclude the rich."[29] Making exceptions to rights, Paine argued, "implies a stigma on the moral character of the persons excluded, and this is what no part of the community has the right to pronounce upon another part."[30]

Equality of rights was commended not only by morality, in Paine's view, but by pragmatic considerations as well. The advantage of equality, Paine proclaimed, is "clear and simple," for "where the rights of man are equal, every man must finally see the necessity of protecting the rights of others as the most effectual security for his own."[31] Warned Paine with noteworthy prescience, "This opinion has already been fatal to thousands, who, not contented with *equal rights*, have sought more till they lost all, and experienced in themselves the degrading *inequality* they endeavored to fix upon others."[32]

Paine thus formulated a clear vision of civil rights as natural rights enshrined in civil law and protected in equal measure for all. For Paine, then, the civil rights vision consisted of two essential components: natural rights and equality of rights.

Other theorists of the revolutionary era echoed Paine's understanding of civil rights. Samuel Adams declared in 1772 that "[e]very natural Right not expressly given up or from the nature of a Social Compact necessarily ceded remains." Expanding upon this theme, Adams argued that

> it is the greatest absurdity to suppose it in the power of one or any number of men at the entering into society, to renounce their essential natural rights ... when the great end of civil government from the very nature of its institution is for the support, protection and defence of those very rights: the principal of which ... are life liberty and property.[33]

Indeed, the concept of civil rights as natural rights enshrined in civil law and protected in equal measure for all provided the moral justification for rebellion against the Crown. As de Tocqueville later observed, "It was the idea of right that enabled men to define anarchy and tyranny."[34] In indicting the tyranny of England, James Otis invoked the concept of civil rights when he declared that "the natural liberty of man is to be free from any superior power on earth, and not to be under the will or legislative authority of man, but only to have the law of nature for his rule." Otis spoke for equality of rights when he protested that Parliament's laws, enforced in oppressive fashion against the colonists, "shall and ought to be equally binding, as upon the subjects of Great Britain within the realm."[35]

These principles were incorporated into the fundamental doctrine of the new nation. The Declaration of Independence, which remains today the most eloquent statement of natural rights ever written, parallels the civil rights construct articulated by Paine and his compatriots. Invoking the "Laws of Nature," the Declaration recites the "self-evident" truths that "all men are created equal" and "endowed by their Creator with certain unalienable Rights," among which are "Life, Liberty and the pursuit of Happiness." In order "to secure these rights, Governments are instituted among Men, deriving their just powers from the consent of the governed."

This was the government the framers of the Constitution set out to establish. For James Madison, civil rights were embodied in the concept of property. Madison declared in his essay on property in 1792 that "[g]overnment is instituted to protect property of every sort," including "that which lies in the various rights of individuals." Madison thus defined property in broad terms:

> In its larger and juster meaning, it embraces every thing to which a man may attach a value and have a right, and *which leaves to every one else the like advantage.* . . . [A] man has a property in his opinions and the free communication of them. He has a property of peculiar value in his religious opinions, and in the profession and practice dictated by them. He has a property very dear to him in the safety and liberty of his person. He has an equal property in the free use of his faculties, and free choice of the objects on which to employ them.[36]

"The protection of these faculties," Madison wrote in *The Federalist* No. 10, "is the first object of government."[37]

The framers determined to protect these rights in two ways: by restricting the power of government (and the ability of special interest groups, or "factions," to exploit that power to the detriment of individual rights), and by providing affirmative protections for those rights. The first goal was accomplished in several ways, including the separation and balance of powers among the various branches of government, and restraints on the influence of special interest groups in the form of the commerce, privileges and immunities, due process, and eminent domain clauses.[38]

The means of accomplishing the second objective, providing safeguards for individual rights, were the subject of controversy, with substantial debate over whether to explicitly enumerate fundamental individual rights in the Constitution. Alexander Hamilton warned that to specify individual rights in a constitution of limited governmental powers would be "dangerous" since it would "declare that things shall not be done which there is no power to do" and thereby "afford a colorable pretext to claim more [powers] than were granted."[39] But the contrary position prevailed, and the original Constitution was amended to specify certain fundamental individual rights in the first eight amendments. The Constitution was further amended to protect the "*residuum* of natural liberty" that was earlier envisioned by Blackstone, with the Ninth Amendment declaring that "[t]he enumeration in the Constitution of certain rights, shall not be construed to deny or disparage others retained by the people"; and the Tenth Amendment establishing that "[t]he powers not delegated to the United States by the Constitution or prohibited by it to the States, are reserved to the States respectively, or to the people."

As Randy Barnett has ably argued, these provisions, particularly the Ninth Amendment, illustrate that the "freedom to act within the boundaries provided by one's common law rights may be viewed as a central background presumption of the Constitution." Accordingly, Barnett concludes, "the Ninth Amendment can be viewed as establishing a general constitutional presumption in favor of individual liberty."[40]

The incorporation of these natural law principles into the basic law of the land marked a seminal event in the quest to protect the basic rights of man. This great promise was in large measure nullified, however, by the sanction conferred upon the institution of slavery by many who asserted these principles. Slavery is the most profound possible departure from the principles of liberty. The tragic compromise of these principles at the time our nation was founded was an error of such magnitude that we have not fully recovered from it today.

Fortunately, many of the founders, including Paine, Benjamin Franklin, Alexander Hamilton, and John Jay, applied these principles and vigorously promoted the abolition of slavery. The great abolitionist leaders who followed, most notably William Lloyd Garrison and Frederick Douglass, consistently invoked natural law principles as the moral justification for their cause.[41] Abraham Lincoln declared that the "entire records of the world . . . may be searched in vain for one single affirmation . . . that the negro was not included in the Declaration of Independence." Slavery, he lamented, "forces so many really good people amongst ourselves into an open war with the very fundamental principles of civil liberty."[42]

Meanwhile, the defenders of slavery rejected natural rights and crafted an alternative ideology based on racial distinctions, paternalism, and majoritarianism. Alexander Stephens, vice president of the Confederacy, defined the terms of the debate:

> The prevailing ideas entertained by . . . most of the leading statesmen at the time of the formation of the old Constitution, were that the enslavement of the African was in violation of the laws of nature: that it was wrong in principle, socially, morally, and politically. . . . Those ideas were fundamentally wrong.[43]

The Civil War was a war for America's soul. The central issue of slavery presented a battle between competing ideologies, with the principles of natural rights on one side and their antithesis on the other. The abolition of slavery marked an epochal triumph for the principles of civil rights and provided an opportunity to revisit— and reconfirm—the original understanding of civil rights.

Indeed, the years immediately following the Civil War were remarkable for the theoretical clarity of the legislative enactments during that period. More than at any time since the framing of the Constitution—indeed, perhaps even more so than then—the lawmakers who passed the civil rights legislation of 1866-1875 and the Thirteenth, Fourteenth, and Fifteenth Amendments were animated by principles, and they possessed the political power to enshrine those principles in law. This phenomenon was made possible by a unique configuration of circumstances: the lawmakers were vindicating principles over which a war was fought and won; moreover, as a result of that war, Congress was dominated as never before by a single political party, and indeed by a radical wing of that party. Almost like a strong majority in a parliamentary system, the radical Republicans were free to change the face of American government in conformity with a clearly defined philosophical vision.

The Fourteenth Amendment's principled heritage would later be denied. Justice Oliver Wendell Holmes, for instance, contended that "a constitution is not intended to embody a particular economic theory, whether of paternalism and the organic relation of the citizen to the state or of *laissez-faire*. . . . The Fourteenth Amendment does not enact Mr. Herbert Spencer's Social Statics."[44] At least insofar as the Fourteenth Amendment is concerned, Justice Holmes was manifestly incorrect. As former Solicitor General Charles Fried observes, Holmes' contention "may be true of other constitutions, but it's not true of ours, which was organized upon very explicit principles of political theory."[45]

The political theory embodied in the Fourteenth Amendment traced its origins to America's foundings and was reinforced by the exigencies of the day. The nullification of basic individual rights epitomized by slavery made the post-Civil War legislators keenly aware of the importance of protecting those rights against future invasions. Moreover, the experience of the "Black Codes" following the war, during which Southern governments attempted to restore a feudal society through indirect means such as restrictions on labor contracts,[46] made it clear that more than the simple abolition of slavery was necessary to protect civil rights.

As a result, the framers of the Civil War amendments set out to bolster and expand upon the protections of fundamental individual rights contained in the original Constitution and Bill of Rights, protecting those rights against the tyranny of the majority effectuated by the coercive power of government. And so they did. Representative William Lawrence exemplified this spirit when he proclaimed that the Civil Rights Act of 1866, the precursor to the Fourteenth Amendment, "is scarcely less to the people of this country than the Magna Charta was to the people of England."[47]

Unlike the original Constitution, which primarily protected civil rights against infringements by the federal government, the new protections were aimed principally at the states, resulting in what Herman Belz calls the "nationalization" of civil rights. And in keeping with the predominant abuses of the times, the protections sought by the amendment's framers, says Belz, were "largely economic in nature."[48] In defining civil rights, he observes, the Reconstruction Congress, like the natural rights theorists of the Revolutionary era, "produced a firm distinction between civil rights on the one hand and political and social rights on the other," and thus "confined their attention to the protection of person and property" in the early civil rights enactments.[49]

Indeed, the framers of the Fourteenth Amendment and related legislation consistently built upon natural rights principles. Bernard Siegan notes that the leaders of the Reconstruction Congress frequently cited Blackstone and Kent as the "foremost legal authorities" in their efforts to strengthen protection for civil rights.[50] Like Kent and Blackstone, they believed that "[n]atural rights were insulated from the majority."[51]

Their views on this issue also closely paralleled those of Herbert Spencer, whose *Social Statics*, published in 1850, built upon the concept of civil rights articulated earlier by Thomas Paine and others. Spencer spoke to both components of the civil rights equation when he declared that the

liberty of each, limited by the like liberties of all, is the rule in conformity with which society must be organized. Freedom being the prerequisite to normal life in the individual, equal freedom becomes the pre-requisite to normal life in society. And if this law of equal freedom is the *primary* law of right relationship between man and man, then no desire to get fulfilled a *secondary* law can warrant us in breaking it.[52]

The leaders of the Reconstruction Congress repeatedly made it plain that they were incorporating natural rights principles into the fundamental law of the land, building upon the existing natural law foundation in the Constitution. Senator Lyman Trumbull, chairman of the Senate Judiciary Committee that framed the Civil Rights Act of 1866, provided the most comprehensive definition of civil rights as natural rights enshrined in civil law, a definition that would inform subsequent legislative enactments throughout the Reconstruction era:

> Natural liberty is defined to be the "Power of acting as one thinks fit, without any restraint or control, unless by the law of nature, being a right inherent in us by birth, and one of the gifts of God to man in his creation, when he imbued him with the faculty of will."
>
> But every man who enters society gives up a part of this natural liberty ... for the advantages he obtains in the protection which civil government gives him. Civil liberty, or the liberty which a person enjoys in society, is thus defined by Blackstone [see earlier citation]. ...
>
> That is the liberty to which every citizen is entitled; that is the liberty that was intended to be secured by the Declaration of Independence and the Constitution of the United States, and more especially by the [Thirteenth] amendment which has recently been adopted.[53]

The framers of the Fourteenth Amendment sought to protect both components of the civil rights equation, fundamental individual rights and equality under law. As historian Michael Kent Curtis observes, these legislators believed that "[g]overnment existed, as the Declaration of Independence asserted, to protect natural rights of man—inalienable rights to life, liberty, and property. Because of the nature of the social compact, all citizens shared their fundamental rights equally."[54] This intention was reflected in the various enactments of the period, which were intended, in the words of Senator Henry Wilson, to ensure the "security of the liberties of all men, and the security of equal, universal, and impartial liberty."[55]

Though the Civil War amendments and related legislation provided the basic tools by which Americans could vindicate their civil rights,* these protections, like those embodied in the original Constitution, were not faithfully implemented in the years following their adoption. A number of factors combined to thwart the great promise of the Reconstruction era: the deaths of abolition leaders, including William Lloyd Garrison; a refocusing of national attention away from civil rights issues, in part because of the corruption of the Grant Administration; and the termination of Reconstruction following the disputed presidential election of 1876.[56]

This erosion of civil rights protections could not have occurred without the abdication by the courts of their role as the ultimate guardian of those rights. This abdication commenced swiftly with the Supreme Court's evisceration of the privileges or immunities clause in the *Slaughter-House Cases* in 1873, and reached its apex with *Plessy* v. *Ferguson* in 1896. These decisions unleashed governments at every level to nullify civil rights in myriad ways, denying those rights particularly to the recently emancipated blacks.

Once again, the foremost advocates of civil rights made their case on the strength of the traditional civil rights vision. Black leaders such as Booker T. Washington and W.E.B. DuBois repeatedly called for individual self-determination.[57] Though DuBois would later turn to socialism, in 1903 he proclaimed in his classic work, *The Souls of Black Folk*, that "[t]here are to-day no truer exponents of the pure human spirit of the Declaration of Independence than the American Negroes."[58] These principles also guided the creation in 1909 of the NAACP, whose founder, Oswald Garrison Villard, demanded "that the colored people shall have every one of the privileges and rights of American citizens." The NAACP adopted a program calling for the "abolition of color-hyphenation and the substitution of straight Americanism," specifically through equal voting rights, equal educational opportunity, fair trials, the right to sit on juries, anti-lynching laws, equal

* The history and meaning of specific provisions of the Fourteenth Amendment will be explored in Parts 2 (privileges or immunities) and 3 (equality under law) of this manuscript.

treatment on public carriers, equal access to tax-supported services, and equal employment opportunities.[59]

The next half century was a difficult one for the civil rights movement, but those who engineered the victories of the 1950s and 1960s faithfully and consistently invoked the principles of natural rights.[60] In his brief for the NAACP in *Brown* v. *Board of Education*, Thurgood Marshall traced the concept of civil rights from its origins in the philosophy of Locke and Thomas Jefferson through the framers of the Fourteenth Amendment, and he relied on this traditional understanding of civil rights to assail the doctrine of "separate but equal."[61] Likewise, James Farmer of the Congress of Racial Equality emphasized the civil rights goals of "total freedom of choice ... throughout American society,"[62] and of equality under law, "color-blindness permeat[ing] the land." This promise, Farmer declared, "has been the nation's implicit ideal since America was a glint in Jefferson's eye. It is nothing but Jeffersonian individualism extended to all people."[63] Senator Hubert Humphrey, the principal sponsor of the Civil Rights Act of 1964, remarked that

> our standard of judgment in the last analysis is not some group's power ... but an *equal* opportunity for *persons*.
>
> Do you want a society that is nothing but an endless power struggle among organized groups? Do you want a society where there is no place for the independent individual? I don't.[64]

But perhaps the most eloquent proponent of the traditional civil rights vision was Martin Luther King, Jr. King firmly aligned himself with "what is best in the American dream" and dedicated himself to the goal of "bringing our nation back to the great wells of democracy which were dug deep by the founding fathers in their formulation of the Constitution and the Declaration of Independence."[65] For King, the Declaration established "that there are certain basic rights that are neither conferred by nor derived from the state," a characteristic that distinguishes America "from systems of government which make the state an end within itself."[66] King brought this understanding to the steps of the Lincoln Memorial when he proclaimed that:

we have come to our nation's Capital to cash a check. When the architects of our republic wrote the magnificent words of the Constitution and the Declaration of Independence, they were signing a promissory note to which every American was to fall heir. This note was a promise that all men would be guaranteed the unalienable rights of life, liberty, and the pursuit of happiness.[67]

The great legislative triumphs of the 1960s—the Civil Rights Act, the Voting Rights Act, and the Twenty-fourth Amendment—placed the finishing touches on the work started by the founders of the American republic and furthered by the framers of the Fourteenth Amendment. All of these constitutional and statutory provisions were intended to secure individuals in their basic rights, with equality under law. All were championed by advocates motivated by the principles of natural rights.

Despite the many setbacks along the way, the traditional American civil rights vision has enjoyed an unparalleled record of success in expanding individual freedom. The principles that formed this vision provided the moral framework for the guarantees of fundamental rights and equality under law in our Constitution. They led America to abolish slavery and to repudiate "separate but equal." They delivered our nation to the threshold of fulfilling for all the great promise of civil rights.

Indeed, that the original vision remained intact from the Revolutionary era through the Reconstruction period all the way to *Brown* v. *Board of Education* and the Civil Rights Act of 1964 is a remarkable tribute to the vitality of the underlying natural rights principles. When we have strayed from those principles, we have seen the greatest abuses of civil rights; when we have maintained fidelity to those principles, we have experienced our greatest triumphs in fulfilling our nation's promise of civil rights.

That assessment remains true today. For the past 25 years, our nation's civil rights policies have been dominated by a very different set of principles. Many of these principles trace their origins to those in our nation's past who have sought to deprive others of basic rights.

Given the demonstrable success of a civil rights vision that is based on the principles of natural rights, why have we abandoned those principles? What is the competing vision that has supplanted it? What are the ramifications of that abandonment? The answers to these questions provide a powerful incentive to restore the quest for civil rights to its original course.

THE REVISED CIVIL RIGHTS AGENDA

The metamorphosis of the civil rights movement following the triumphs of the 1960s occurred with head-spinning swiftness. The forces contributing to the adoption of a revised civil rights agenda were multiple and complex,[68] reflecting the broader social upheaval of that decade. The reactionary backlash by whites against the modest demands of blacks spawned resentment, polarization, and widespread cynicism about traditional American ideals, a cynicism reinforced by the war in Vietnam.

Probably the strongest pressure to abandon traditional strategies and ideals came from the fact that nothing immediately changed following the victory of the civil rights revolution. Blacks did not suddenly improve their material status, live in the same neighborhoods as whites, or win election to office in large numbers. After two centuries of subjugation and exclusion, many blacks understandably were not content to reap the gradual benefits flowing from the guarantee of baseline opportunities. This frustration was fueled by the black separatist movement, which promised immediate gains. To compete with the separatists for grassroots support, the mainstream civil rights leadership was forced to adopt results-oriented strategies.

A second factor was the growing political influence of that mainstream leadership. Traditionally, the civil rights movement sought to *restrict* the power of government; following the Civil War, the abolitionists used their political power to that end. But the civil rights leadership elite during the 1960s flexed its new-found political muscle in different ways, delivering tangible benefits to its perceived constituency. As civil rights movement veteran Morris Abram would later observe, the movement "turned away from its original principled campaign for equal justice under law to engage in an open contest for social and economic benefits conferred on the basis of race or other classifications previously thought to be invidious."[69]

As Bayard Rustin described it, the "civil rights movement is evolving from a protest movement into a full-fledged *social movement*—an evolution calling its very name into question."[70] This movement seeks ambitious goals such as the redistribution of wealth. As Rustin revealed, "How are these radical objectives to be achieved? The answer is simple, deceptively so—*through political power*."[71] Though taking note of the "strong moralistic strain in the civil rights movement which reminds us that power corrupts," Rustin dismissed that concern since that view "is waning."[72] In this way, the 200-year quest for universal rights was reduced to the status of a special interest lobby; its dynamic leadership transformed itself into an establishment seeking to perpetuate its existence and to expand its power.

These civil rights revisionists introduced three key concepts that laid the foundation for their policy prescriptions. The central theme was the redefinition of "equality" from equal treatment to equal outcomes. As Morris Abram recalls, "During the late 1960s, the civil rights community began to splinter and, certainly by the mid-1970s, much of its leadership had become preoccupied with equality of *results*."[73] Accordingly, Abram explains, a "large segment of the civil rights lobby has turned from the struggle for equality in civil and political rights to the advocacy of redistribution of economic and social rights. And it has made support for the redistribution of these rights as a precondition for being part of the movement."[74]

The second element of the revisionists' conceptual construct was that civil rights inhered not in individuals, but in *groups*. Since past civil rights deprivations were often visited upon people on the basis of their race, the revisionists reasoned that appropriate remedies must speak also to victims as members of disadvantaged groups. Bayard Rustin described this departure from "classical" principles as a "victory of the concept of collective struggle over individual achievement as the road to Negro freedom."[75]

The combined concepts of equality in results and group rights produced a new definition of discrimination. Previously understood as different treatment of individuals on the basis of their race or other irrelevant characteristics, discrimination was now defined to include any instances of different outcomes for different groups.

As Jesse Jackson explained it, "Equality can be measured. It can be turned into numbers."[76] Casting aside the "superficial 'equality of opportunity' that gets so much lip service," Whitney Young argued that the "measure of equality has to be group achievement: when, in each group in our society, roughly the same proportion of people succeed and fail, then we will have true equality."[77]

The third key concept was the abandonment of natural rights in favor of entitlements. Rather than the rights to life, liberty, and property, the new civil rights orthodoxy demanded that government provide certain material benefits to everyone. Whitney Young, for example, would speak of "family allowances ... *as a matter of right*," guaranteed minimum incomes as a "*right* to which people are entitled," and "every family's *right* to a decent home."[78]

These concepts translated into a public policy agenda based on the redistribution of wealth and opportunities. In *The Other America*, Michael Harrington divided America into two parts: the first an "affluent society," which enjoys the "highest standard of life the world has ever known"; and the second "a culture of poverty," which is "beyond history, beyond progress, sunk in a paralyzing, maiming routine."[79] The poor, Harrington asserted, "are so submerged in their poverty that one cannot begin to think about free choice. ... [S]ociety must help them before they can help themselves."[80] Harrington concluded that "[t]here is only one institution in society capable of acting to abolish poverty. That is the Federal Government."[81]

The vision of Harrington and his like-minded allies resulted in a number of now-familiar policy innovations: racial quotas, minority business set-asides, forced busing, and the expansion of welfare entitlements. Moreover, these policies were quickly extended beyond blacks to encompass groups for whom no plausible case for reparations could be made.

These policies and the concepts upon which they rested required a major departure from traditional civil rights principles. As with the pro-slavery apologists, it was not enough for the revisionists merely to argue against those principles. To stake any claim to the moral high ground, the revisionists had to construct an alternative theory of rights, of the proper relationship among individuals, and of the role of the state.

A number of such theories were supplied, but perhaps none so comprehensive and potent as John Rawls' *A Theory of Justice* (1971) and Ronald Dworkin's *Taking Rights Seriously* (1977). Rawls and Dworkin invoke familiar terms such as liberty, equality, and the social contract, but they recast these terms in such a way as to foster a forced egalitarian society.

In Rawls' social compact, individuals do not agree to surrender an insubstantial portion of their rights in the state of nature so as to protect maximum liberty, but rather to restrict their liberty more broadly in ways that yield advantages to all members of society. Specifically, each person will receive a fair share of the benefits of society in accordance with a general conception of justice.[82] For Rawls, a just society is one in which "[a]ll social primary goods—liberty and opportunity, income and wealth, and the bases of self-respect—are to be distributed equally unless an unequal distribution of any or all of these goods is to the advantage of the least favored."[83]

This general conception of justice is guided by two principles. The first is the equal right to certain liberties, which Rawls defines as political liberty, freedom of speech and assembly, liberty of conscience and freedom of thought, freedom of the person along with the right to hold personal property, and freedom from arbitrary arrest and seizure.[84] The second principle involves the "arrangement" of social and economic inequalities in a fair manner. A fair arrangement cannot rely on the free market and a guarantee of equal treatment, Rawls argues, since those mechanisms fail to "mitigate the influence of social contingencies and natural misfortune on distributive shares."[85] Accordingly, "in order to treat all persons equally, to provide genuine equality of opportunity, society must give more attention to those with fewer native assets and to those born into less favorable social positions."[86] Hence, guaranteeing certain essential liberties and arranging opportunities to accommodate those who could not achieve their share of social goods on the basis of equal treatment alone will produce a society in which all members share equally in those social goods.

Like Rawls, Ronald Dworkin developed a rights-based theory, but he emphasizes the fundamental right to equality. Dworkin agrees that individuals possess certain liberties such as those listed in the Bill of Rights along with the right to make personal moral decisions, but he contends that these rights "are derivative, not from a more abstract general right to liberty as such, but from the right to equality itself."[87] This right to equality is not a right to equal treatment, Dworkin argues, but a right to be treated as an equal, which means the right "to be treated with the same respect and concern as anyone else." Dworkin applies a utilitarian standard in enforcing this right. "An individual's right to be treated as an equal means that his potential loss must be treated as a matter of concern, but that loss may nevertheless be outweighed by the gain to the community as a whole."[88]

Dworkin applies this equality standard to the case of Marco DeFunis, a white student who was excluded from the University of Washington law school pursuant to a racial quota.[89] According to Dworkin, DeFunis's right to be treated as an equal means "he has a right that his interests be treated as fully and sympathetically as the interests of any others when the law school decides whether to count race as a pertinent criterion for admission."[90] Taking race into account is no more a differential criterion than taking intelligence into account, Dworkin reasons, but the former has the possible benefit of making "the community more equal overall," thus justifying the burden placed on DeFunis.[91]

The overall conceptual framework created by the civil rights revisionists and their intellectual allies is fatally flawed for several reasons. First, the standards the revisionists attempt to apply, particularly Dworkin's concept of equality, are hopelessly subjective. The traditional civil rights vision relies on the objective standard of equal treatment. As Paine argued, a major benefit of this standard is that every individual is self-interested in honoring it: the standard cannot survive if it is compromised in any instance, and the individual who benefits from its compromise in one instance cannot tell whether he or she will be the victim next. By transforming equality into a subjective standard, the concept is reduced to a spoils system, and an individual's support for equality will depend on whose ox is gored. Any concept of equality that departs from equal treatment ultimately disintegrates into exploitation of some individuals by others.

Similarly, an "objective" definition of equality that purports to ensure equal outcomes rather than equal treatment is inherently incompatible with individual liberty. The equal treatment standard makes possible maximum liberty for everyone because it establishes the boundary as the right of all others to equal liberty. As Friedrich Hayek explains, "From the fact that people are very different it follows that, if we treat them equally, the result must be inequality in their actual position, and that the only way to place them in an equal position would be to treat them differently." Equal outcomes thus require "discriminatory coercion," which violates both equal treatment and individual liberty. Concludes Hayek, "Equality before the law and material equality are therefore not only different but are in conflict with each other; and we can achieve either the one or the other, but not both at the same time."[92] Given those two paths, the better choice is obvious: liberty can lead to material progress and even to equality of outcomes, but coerced material outcomes by definition can never lead to liberty.

A second major flaw of this alternative civil rights vision is that it sacrifices the individual to the group, suppressing the value of the individual persona in much the same way as did the institution of slavery. Whatever rationales can justify favorable treatment of people by virtue of their membership in particular groups can also justify adverse treatment of individuals by virtue of their group identification. Only a system of rights inhering in every individual can provide durable safeguards against majoritarian tyranny.

Finally, the revised civil rights agenda has shifted from the assertion of absolute rights to a negotiation of entitlements.[93] In so doing, it necessarily compromises the inalienability of rights and thereby reduces their value. For instance, the equal opportunity of every individual is compromised in favor of racial quotas in the workplace and forced racial balance in the schools; similarly, rent control destroys the inalienability of property rights and thereby diminishes their exchange value. Rather than an individual rights-based construct, which tends to elevate individual rights to the highest common denominator, the revisionists' construct is a leveling philosophy, which cares not at all about the extent of opportunities that are available so long as the results are evenly distributed.

Of course, no such even distribution has occurred. Although the revisionists' construct has dominated federal civil rights policy for the past 25 years, the promised racial parity has not taken place. In fact, perhaps the most perverse by-product of the abandonment of traditional civil rights principles in favor of a results-oriented agenda is that we are perhaps further away from equality of results than we were when the nation was plunged into this quagmire a quarter century ago.[94]

This does not mean that the revisionists are without strong arguments to support their cause. Among the most compelling is that since past deprivations of civil rights were inflicted on groups rather than individuals, remedies (including reparations) ought to be defined in group terms as well. This argument makes logical sense, but it suffers two fatal flaws. First, such a remedy by definition requires discrimination, often in favor of non-victims and at the expense of those who are guilty of no wrongdoing. Second, group-based entitlements fail to truly remedy unequal education and entry-level job opportunities. Hence such remedies leave the most disadvantaged no better equipped to enjoy the benefits of a free society than before.

Certainly, the past quarter century has witnessed enormous progress by many individuals who are members of groups that suffered past (and often present) discrimination. But the evidence suggests that such progress has resulted not from outcomes-oriented mechanisms such as racial quotas, business set-asides, and forced busing, but rather from opportunity-oriented factors such as education and economic growth.[95]

Indeed, coercive results-oriented strategies have proven little more than surface-level solutions to contemporary social problems, leaving unaddressed such debilitating problems as welfare dependency and poor urban education. These burdens disproportionately afflict the poorest members of society, while results-oriented strategies tend to benefit those who need help the least. In *The Truly Disadvantaged*, William Julius Wilson, a liberal sociologist from the University of Chicago, chronicles the "growing economic schism between lower-income and higher-income black families," finding that for millions among the largely black underclass, "the past three decades have been a time of regression, not progress."[96] These dismal conclusions were largely echoed in the report in 1989 of the Committee on the Status of Black Americans.[97]

Wilson found that "the factors associated with the growing woes of low-income blacks are exceedingly complex and go beyond the issue of contemporary discrimination."[98] Results-oriented civil rights policies, Wilson reveals, have tended to exacerbate income differences among blacks. "Race-specific policies," Wilson observes, are "beneficial to more advantaged blacks," but "do little for those who are truly disadvantaged."[99]

Even when measured by its own standards, then, the revisionists' civil rights agenda is an unequivocal failure. Yet the single-minded zeal with which that agenda is promoted by the civil rights leadership elite makes meaningful discussion of alternatives difficult. This phenomenon is particularly unfortunate in light of current economic and demographic circumstances: even as the numbers of the underclass multiply, companies around the country are facing severe shortages of skilled labor. Numbers-oriented strategies have done little to bridge the skills, information, and culture gap that separates the economically disadvantaged from these employment opportunities. We have today an opportunity perhaps unparalleled in history to make the American Dream a reality for millions who are currently outside the economic mainstream; yet instead of crafting effective "affirmative action" strategies designed to give real tools to the disadvantaged,[100] the debate has failed to progress beyond the abyss of quotas.

But surely the most tragic consequence of the abandonment of traditional civil rights principles is the continued existence— some would say an exacerbation—of racial polarization among Americans. As Nathan Glazer recounts, the revisionists' civil rights construct arrested the emergence of a new "pattern of dealing with ethnic differences" in America, one which does not give [such differences] formal acknowledgement, neither encourages nor discourages group allegiance and identification, and treats every individual as an individual and not as a member of a group. This is now threatened by public policies which emphasize rigid lines of division between ethnic groups and make the ethnic characteristics of individuals, because of public determinations, primary for their personal fate.[101]

The redefinition of civil rights from those basic rights we all share as Americans into special burdens for some and privileges for others has destroyed the precious yet fragile consensus that supported the civil rights triumphs of the 1960s. Morris Abram charges that the civil rights establishment, by shifting the focus from opportunity to social engineering, has lost "the support of moderate Americans, both black and white, who sustained the movement from the outset."[102]

Representative John Lewis (D-GA), a veteran of the civil rights movement, summarized succinctly the nature of the present crisis: "I don't think the movement as a whole has ever reclaimed its focus and its sense of moral authority and . . . moral leadership since the assassination of Martin Luther King, Jr."[103] The quest for civil rights in America has been cast adrift, its future course uncharted, and its moral leadership unclaimed.

A PRINCIPLED NEW COURSE FOR CIVIL RIGHTS

After two centuries of incremental but steady progress in securing civil rights for all Americans, the past quarter century has been a time of confusion and regression, marked by a wholesale abandonment of the fundamental principles of civil rights by many people who claim to lead the fight for civil rights. The contemporary civil rights establishment has sacrificed the civil rights movement's greatest goals by exchanging individual freedom for group entitlements, equality of opportunity for forced equality of results, and dignity for dependency.

The seeds of our present morass were planted more than 200 years ago, when many of our nation's creators found reasons to make exceptions to the universal principles of civil rights. We have paid the price ever since. We have found that adherence to the natural law principles of civil rights means greater liberty for everyone and that departures from those principles, no matter how benevolent the justification, means a restriction of liberty for everyone.

These lessons of history suggest a definite course of action: a return to the basic principles of civil rights, applied in a consistent and aggressive manner to eradicate those remaining arbitrary barriers that separate individuals from opportunities. A strategy to promote individual empowerment would do a great deal for the Ego Browns and the Mark Anthony Nevelses of the world—not merely by securing the right to shine shoes on public streets or to attend a neighborhood public school, but by securing the opportunity to partake in the blessings of American liberty.

Indeed, the beauty of a civil rights strategy that stands shoulder to shoulder with Ego Brown and Mark Anthony Nevels is that it returns to the spirit that made the civil rights movement great—the American spirit. Unlike the current civil rights agenda that divides Americans, a strategy that focuses on individual empowerment draws upon the principles and values that bind us together.

Can we do it? Of course we can. For the business we are about is nothing less than fulfilling the mission of our nation's heritage. Such a noble quest requires a keen understanding of the true meaning of civil rights, plus an unyielding commitment to fundamental principles.

We would do well to take as our credo the fiery declaration of William Lloyd Garrison, who launched his 35-year crusade for the abolition of slavery with this vow:

> I will be as harsh as truth, and as uncompromising as justice. On this subject, I do not wish to think, or speak, or write, with moderation. No! No! Tell a man whose house is on fire to give a moderate alarm; tell him to moderately rescue his wife from the hands of the ravisher; tell the mother to gradually extricate her babe from the fire into which it has fallen—but urge me not to use moderation in a cause like the present. I am in earnest—I will not equivocate—I will not excuse—I will not retreat a single inch—AND I WILL BE HEARD.[104]

Garrison's tone of urgency 160 years ago is appropriate to our own age. Let's reinvigorate our spirit with first principles and move forward in the quest to fulfill America's promise of civil rights.

ENDNOTES

1. *Brown* v. *Barry*, 710 F.Supp. 352 (D.D.C. 1989).
2. Robert Safian, "Civil Rights, Conservative Style," *American Lawyer* (May 1989): 129.
3. *Brown* v. *Barry*, 710 F. Supp. 352 (D.D.C. 1989). This lawsuit was the first triumph for the Landmark Legal Foundation Center for Civil Rights.
4. See Mary Chlopecki, "It's Illegal to Shine in D.C.," *Conservative Digest* (November 1988): 74.
5. Landmark Legal Foundation filed a motion challenging this policy on behalf of black schoolchildren in *Jenkins* v. *State of Missouri*, No. 77–0420–CV–W–4 (D. Mo.) (motion to modify on behalf of Ronika Newton et al., filed 13 July 1989).
6. Abram, p. 1326 (emphasis in original).
7. Robert Detlefsen, "Triumph of the Race-Conscious State: The Politics of Civil Rights, 1980–86," doctoral dissertation, University of California–Berkeley, 1988, p. 21.
8. Otto Gierke, *Natural Law and the Theory of Society 1500 to 1800* (Boston: Beacon Press, 1957), p. 113, note 112.
9. *Id.*, p. 112.
10. *Id.*, p. 113.
11. *Id.*
12. John Locke, *Second Treatise of Government* (Indianapolis: Hackett Publishing Co., 1980), p. 9.
13. See Bernard Siegan, *The Supreme Court's Constitution* (New Brunswick, N.J.: Transaction Books, 1987), p. 78.
14. William Blackstone, "Commentaries." In *The Founders' Constitution*, vol. 5, edited by Philip B. Kurland and Ralph Lerner, p. 389. Chicago: University of Chicago Press, 1987.
15. *Id.*, p. 388.
16. *Id.*
17. *Id.*, p. 389.
18. *Id.*, p. 388.
19. *Id.*, p. 389.
20. Eric Foner, "Tom Paine's Republic: Radical Ideology and Social Change." In *The American Revolution*, edited by Alfred F. Young, p. 189. DeKalb, Ill.: Northern Illinois University Press, 1976.
21. *Id.*, p. 199.
22. Thomas Paine, "The Rights of Man." In *Thomas Paine*, edited by Harry Hayden Clark, p. 89. New York: Hill and Wang, 1961.

23. *Id.*, p. 88.
24. *Id.*, p. 89.
25. Thomas Paine, "A Serious Address to the People of Pennsylvania." In *Burke and Paine on Revolution and the Rights of Man*, edited by Robert B. Dishman, p. 198, note 2. New York: Charles Scribner's Sons, 1971.
26. Thomas Paine, "Dissertation on the First Principles of Government." In Dishman, *id.*, p. 200.
27. *Id.*, p. 199.
28. *Id.*, p. 196.
29. *Id.*
30. *Id.*, p. 198.
31. *Id.*, p. 201.
32. *Id.*, p. 197.
33. Samuel Adams, "The Rights of the Colonists." In Kurland and Lerner, p. 395.
34. Alexis de Tocqueville, *Democracy in America*, vol. I (New York: Vintage Books, 1945), p. 254.
35. James Otis, "The Rights of the British Colonies Asserted and Proved." In Samuel Eliot Morison, ed., *Sources and Documents Illustrating the American Revolution and the Formation of the Federal Constitution*, 2d ed. (London: Oxford University Press, 1970), p. 5.
36. James A. Dorn, "Judicial Protection of Economic Liberties." In *Economic Liberties and the Judiciary*, edited by James A. Dorn and Henry G. Manne, p. 3. Fairfax, Va.: George Mason University Press, 1987.
37. *The Federalist*, no. 10 (Madison).
38. See Jonathan R. Macey, "Promoting Public-Regarding Legislation Through Statutory Interpretation: An Interest Group Model," 86 *Colum. L. Rev.* 223 (1986).
39. *The Federalist*, no. 84 (Hamilton).
40. Randy E. Barnett, "Reconceiving the Ninth Amendment," 74 *Cornell L. Rev.* 1, 35 (1988).
41. Bolick, *Changing Course*, pp. 18–23.
42. Terry Eastland and William J. Bennett, *Counting by Race* (New York: Basic Books, 1979), p. 47.
43. *Id.*, p. 55.
44. *Lochner* v. *New York*, 198 U.S. 45, 75 (1905) (Holmes, J., dissenting).

45. "Crisis in the Courts," *Manhattan Report on Economic Policy*, vol. V, no. 2 (1982), p. 4.
46. See Robert Higgs, *Competition and Competition* (Cambridge, England: Cambridge University Press, 1977), p. 7.
47. *Cong. Globe*, 39th Cong., 1st Sess., H. p. 1833 (1866).
48. Herman Belz, *Emancipation and Equal Rights: Politics and Constitutionalism in the Civil War Era* (New York: W. W. Norton & Co., 1978), p. 109.
49. *Id.*, p. 116.
50. Bernard H. Siegan, "Economic Liberties and the Constitution: Protection at the State Level." In Dorn and Manne, p. 141.
51. Siegan, *The Supreme Court's Constitution*, p. 59.
52. Herbert Spencer, "Social Statics." In *Selected Works of Herbert Spencer* (New York: D. Appleton and Company, 1892), p. 45.
53. *Cong. Globe*, 39th Cong., 1st Sess., 1866, Senate, pp. 474–75.
54. Michael Kent Curtis, *No State Shall Abridge* (Durham, N.C.: Duke University Press, 1986), p. 41.
55. *Cong. Globe*, 39th Cong., 1st Sess., 1866, S. p. 111.
56. Bolick, *Changing Course*, p. 27.
57. *Id.*, pp. 37–39.
58. W.E.B. DuBois, *The Souls of Black Folk* (Millwood, N.Y.: Kraus-Thomson Organization Ltd., 1973), p. 11.
59. Bolick, *Changing Course*, pp. 39–40.
60. *Id.*, pp. 31–52.
61. *Id.*, p. 45.
62. James Farmer, "Freedom—When?" In *The Civil Rights Reader*, edited by Leon Friedman, p. 129. New York: Walker and Company, 1967.
63. *Id.*, p. 125.
64. Abram, p. 1322.
65. Martin Luther King, Jr., "Letter from a Birmingham Jail." In *The Negro in American History*, vol. I, edited by Mortimer J. Adler, p. 195. Chicago: Encyclopedia Britannica Educational Corp., 1969.
66. Taylor Branch, "Uneasy Holiday," *The New Republic*, 3 February 1986, p. 27.
67. Martin Luther King, Jr., "I Have a Dream." In Friedman, pp. 110–111.
68. See Bolick, *Changing Course*, pp. 53–55. A number of recent books have explored this remarkable period of American history. Among these are Taylor Branch, *Parting the Waters* (New York: Simon and Schuster, 1988); Abigail M. Thernstrom, *Whose Votes Count?*

(Cambridge: Harvard University Press, 1987); David J. Garrow, *Bearing the Cross* (New York: William Morrow and Co., 1986); Juan Williams, *Eyes on the Prize* (New York: Viking, 1986); Harold Cruse, *Plural But Equal* (New York: William Morrow and Co., 1987); Ralph David Abernathy; *And the Walls Came Tumbling Down* (New York: Harper and Row, 1989).

69.   Abram, p. 1312.

70.   Bayard Rustin, *Down the Line* (Chicago: Quadrangle Books, 1971), p. 115 [emphasis supplied].

71.   *Id.*, p. 118 [emphasis supplied].

72.   *Id.*

73.   Abram, p. 1313 [emphasis supplied].

74.   *Id.*, p. 1325.

75.   Bolick, *Changing Course*, p. 58.

76.   Eastland and Bennett, p. 7.

77.   Whitney M. Young, Jr., *Beyond Racism* (New York: McGraw-Hill Book Co., 1969), p. 152.

78.   Young, pp. 176, 179, and 183 [emphasis supplied].

79.   Michael Harrington, *The Other America* (Baltimore: Penguin Books, 1963), p. 159.

80.   *Id.*, p. 162.

81.   *Id.*, p. 171.

82.   John Rawls, *A Theory of Justice* (Cambridge, Mass.: Belknap Press, 1971), p. 112.

83.   *Id.*, p. 303.

84.   *Id.*, pp. 60–61.

85.   *Id.*, p. 73.

86.   *Id.*, p. 100.

87.   Ronald Dworkin, *Taking Rights Seriously* (London: Gerald Duckworth and Co., 1977), p. xiii.

88.   *Id.*, p. 227.

89.   See *DeFunis* v. *Odegaard*, 416 U.S. 312 (1974).

90.   Dworkin, p. 227.

91.   *Id.*, p. 228.

92.   F. A. Hayek, *The Constitution of Liberty* (Chicago: University of Chicago Press, 1960), p. 87.

93.   I am indebted to Steven Eagle for this insight.

94.   See Bolick, *Changing Course*, pp. 84–90.

95.   See, e.g., James P. Smith and Finis R. Welch, *Closing the Gap: Forty Years of Economic Progress for Blacks* (Santa Monica, Cal.: Rand Corp., 1986). For an insightful analysis of the perverse effects

of supposedly beneficent government policies on the poor, see Charles Murray, *Losing Ground* (New York: Basic Books, 1984).

96. William Julius Wilson, *The Truly Disadvantaged* (Chicago: University of Chicago Press, 1987), p. 110.

97. Gerald David Jaynes and Robin M. Williams, Jr., eds., *A Common Destiny: Blacks and American Society* (Washington: National Academy Press, 1989).

98. Wilson, p. 110.

99. *Id.*

100. See, e.g., Bolick and Nestleroth, pp. 65–97.

101. Glazer, p. 70.

102. Abram, p. 1325.

103. "Where Did the Civil Rights Movement Go Wrong?" *Human Rights* (Fall 1988): 22.

104. Archibald A. Grimke, *William Lloyd Garrison* (New York: Negro Universities Press, 1969), p. 117.

Part II

PROTECTING FUNDAMENTAL INDIVIDUAL RIGHTS: DISMANTLING LIBERTY'S *SLAUGHTER-HOUSE*

[T]he task of creating what I might call a constitutional ethos of economic liberty is no easy one. But it is the first task.
                                                            —*Antonin Scalia*[1]

That only is a free government, in the American sense of the term, under which the inalienable right of every citizen to pursue his happiness is unrestrained, except by just, equal, and impartial laws.
                                                            —*Justice Stephen Field*[2]

Alfredo Santos is a born-again capitalist. Once an organizer for farm union leader Cesar Chavez, Santos discovered the benefits of the free-enterprise system during a visit to Mexico City.

It was there Santos discovered the *pesero*—small vans carrying passengers along fixed routes for a flat fee. The service was popular, efficient, and, by all appearances, profitable.

Santos, then a taxicab driver, decided to import the idea to Houston, calling the *pesero* by its American name—"jitney." Using his taxicab during off-duty hours, Santos inaugurated a jitney route in a poor, predominantly Hispanic neighborhood in which public bus service was inadequate and many people couldn't afford cars. Santos offered his service for a flat fee of one dollar, with pickup and discharge of passengers anywhere along the five-mile route.

47

Advertising his service with Spanish-language flyers, Santos quickly developed a booming business, and other off-duty cab drivers soon followed his lead. The jitney was cheaper than a taxicab and much more convenient than a bus, and passengers were delighted to have a transportation option.

Everyone seemed to benefit. But that didn't deter the city's cab inspectors, who threatened to fine Santos for violating the Houston Anti-Jitney Law of 1924. It seems that in the early 1920s, the streetcar industry mounted a highly successful nationwide campaign to eradicate the jitneys, their main source of competition. Sixty-five years later, the streetcar industry was long-since defunct, but the laws remained. And so Santos had to shut down his thriving little business.

Santos tried unsuccessfully to have the law overturned through the legislative process. When those attempts failed, he turned to the courts;[3] but it remains to be seen whether the judiciary will come to the aid of this man who exemplifies the American entrepreneurial spirit.

THE MEANING OF CIVIL RIGHTS

Not all the newcomers to America's shores brought with them great riches, nor did they immediately find riches here. Rather, what generations of immigrants found—what they sought in coming to America—was freedom and opportunity. Essential to this opportunity were the freedoms to obtain and exchange property, to bargain freely over wages and the terms and conditions of employment, and to pursue an occupation or business of the individual's choosing.* These rights might be summarized as "empowerment" rights—the rights mandated by human nature for the sustenance of life.

Those newcomers who eventually have reaped the benefits of the American system, for themselves or for their children, have not done so through racial quotas, contract set-asides, or dependence on welfare. To the contrary, Charles Murray has ably documented that the growth of the welfare state has led to a decline in socio-

---

*These freedoms, of course, were denied to blacks first by the institution of slavery and later by the Jim Crow laws. Other individuals also have suffered deprivations of these rights on account of their race, ethnicity, or gender.

economic advances for minorities and the poor.[4] Rather, those who successfully entered the economic mainstream traditionally did so either through labor, entrepreneurship, education, or a combination of those. Such individuals typically have climbed the rungs of the economic ladder one step at a time, moving closer with each step to attaining the American Dream.

That dream is what motivates individuals like Ego Brown and Alfredo Santos. They ask not for a handout, or a subsidy, or preferential treatment. They do not seek a "safety net" if they fail, although they intend fully to reap the rewards if they succeed. In essence, all they ask for is the basic opportunity that is every American's birthright, every American's civil right.

But when people like Ego Brown and Alfredo Santos seek that opportunity today, often they find their paths blocked by an array of obstacles. Inner-city youngsters, for instance, are by virtue of the public school monopoly often consigned to inferior schools in which educational opportunities are far more scarce than drugs and violence.*[5] Likewise, entry into occupations and businesses— and the freedom to bargain over wages and the terms and conditions of employment—is routinely restricted by a variety of regulations imposed by every level of government. In essence, government is slowly cutting off the bottom rungs of the economic ladder, leaving those outside the economic mainstream to argue their case for quotas and set-asides or to join the welfare rolls.

Many might not think of the plights of Ego Brown and Alfredo Santos in the context of civil rights. But the civil rights laws were precisely intended to protect the rights of property, free labor, and entrepreneurship. Indeed, a major source of contemporary confusion about civil rights is that the civil rights establishment has lost sight of these basic rights.

Most attention in the area of civil rights during the past two centuries has focused on the "equality under law" half of the civil rights equation, rather than on the substantive rights themselves. The reason for this emphasis is simple: the gravest civil rights deprivations in our nation have consisted of the exclusion of people from rights on the basis of immutable characteristics such

*The following section addresses challenging barriers to equal educational opportunities as part of a civil rights strategy that is based on individual empowerment.

as race or color. Consequently, much of civil rights jurisprudence has focused not on securing fundamental rights for individuals, but on protecting individuals against invidious discrimination.

This phenomenon has produced two significant side effects. First, it has allowed some commentators, particularly among conservatives, to view the quest for civil rights *solely* in terms of a battle against discrimination.[6] Such an approach tends to overlook a vital component of civil rights. As Alfred Avins, a leading scholar of legislation in the Reconstruction era, notes, the framers of the Fourteenth Amendment intended to "confer certain civil or natural rights on all persons, white as well as black, and not merely to abolish racial discrimination against Negroes."[7] With the emphasis during the past century on equality of rights, we have tended to overlook the underlying rights themselves.

Meanwhile, this tendency by some to ignore the substantive rights conferred by the civil rights laws has allowed other commentators, particularly on the left end of the political spectrum, to redefine those rights. As James Dorn remarks, this view embraces "a system of justice based on ... notions of social or distributive justice rather than on protection of private property and freedom of contract."[8] We can restore civil rights to their true meaning and effectively make progress in better securing them only if we return to the origins of civil rights and pursue a forward-looking strategy to expand individual empowerment.

Indeed, what the architects of the American civil rights vision had in mind was the right of individuals to control their own destinies. And the framers of both our original Constitution and the Fourteenth Amendment intended to incorporate that vision into the basic law of the land.

This vision was articulated by Sir William Blackstone in his definition of civil liberty, which was often invoked by the founders of the American republic. Blackstone defined civil liberty as "no other than natural liberty so far restrained by human laws (and no farther) as is necessary and expedient for the general advantage of the publick."[9] Civil liberty under this definition thus consists of the freedom of individuals to determine their own affairs free from arbitrary or excessive interference. Friedrich Hayek notes that such a concept of liberty may be characterized as "negative,"

> in the sense that peace is also a negative concept or that security or quiet or the absence of any particular impediment or evil is negative. It is to this class of concepts that liberty belongs: it describes the absence of a particular obstacle—coercion by other men. It becomes positive only through what we make of it.[10]

What specific fundamental individual rights—or "civil rights"— did the framers ascribe to man in a state of civil liberty? According to Herman Belz, the predominant understanding of civil rights

> consisted in the right of all citizens, equally and without hindrance from government, to move about, work and enjoy the rewards of labor, own or rent property, make contracts and participate in the market place, bring suit and testify in courts of law, maintain whatever religious beliefs and practices one wished, and enjoy the benefits of marriage and the family.[11]

These rights, Belz stresses, were "largely economic in nature."[12] Indeed, James Madison emphasized economic liberties when he declared,

> That is not a just government, nor is property secure under it, where arbitrary restrictions, exemptions, and monopolies deny to part of its citizens that free use of their faculties, and free choice of their occupations, which not only constitute their property in the general sense of the word; but are the means of acquiring property strictly so called.[13]

Nonetheless, of all our civil rights as originally defined, economic liberties are today the least protected; indeed, they are particularly singled out by the judiciary as entitled to virtually no protection.* This development is especially remarkable given that

---

*To a significant extent, this is true also of private property rights, which are the subject of an effort similar to this, which will be published in due course by the Pacific Research Institute. Accordingly, this manuscript deals only peripherally with private property rights, though such rights are certainly within the scope of civil rights.

the protection of basic economic liberty—the freedom to pursue a business or profession free from arbitrary or excessive governmental interference—was a foremost concern and objective of the framers of the Fourteenth Amendment. The judicial nullification of economic liberty stands as one of the most pervasive and debilitating deprivations of civil rights in America today.

Efforts to revive economic liberty as a fundamental civil right are not without their detractors. Defenders of extreme judicial deference to the other branches of government would deny courts their central role in protecting economic liberty.[14] William Eaton, for instance, charges that "[n]owhere does the Constitution refer to any concept remotely representing the Liberty of Contract dogma which Louis Lochner wished the Court to impose."*[15] During the "substantive due process" era, in which the Supreme Court sometimes struck down legislation that violated basic economic liberties, Eaton complains, as if it were universally objectionable, that "President Franklin Roosevelt's New Deal found itself tied up in a judicial straitjacket."[16] Yet even Eaton concedes that "[w]hat the framers did intend to protect were such rights as the right to contract [and] to hold property,"[17] although he would apparently deny the judiciary a role in protecting those rights regardless of the framers' intent.

The better view is expressed by Bernard Siegan. "The usual grievance against the Court relates to its excesses—creating powers and rights—usually criticized as judicial activism," observes Siegan, but "[f]ailure to implement existing rights is no less an error than enforcing non-existent rights."[18] Indeed, with respect to the substantive rights protections of the Fourteenth Amendment, the jurisprudence of the last half century is a saga of shameful judicial abdication, with staggering ramifications for society as a whole and for its individual constituents.

Regardless of one's position on judicial restraint versus prin-

*See also the discussion of *Lochner* v. *New York* later in this section.

cipled judicial action,[19] a thorough review of the legislative history of the Fourteenth Amendment reveals a number of important points:

- The broad wording of the Fourteenth Amendment was intended to more explicitly incorporate into the Constitution a well-defined theory of natural law.
- Congress clearly intended the Fourteenth Amendment to protect certain substantive rights—including those enumerated by the Bill of Rights and in the Civil Rights Act of 1866 but also extending to unenumerated natural rights—and to operate as a direct restraint on the power of states to circumvent those rights.
- These rights were designed to be self-executing (i.e., not dependent upon further legislative action) and enforced by the judiciary.
- Although the desire to protect the civil rights of blacks was paramount, the rights embodied in the Fourteenth Amendment are universal and thus extend to all individuals, regardless of race.
- The framers were motivated in large part by the desire to protect economic liberty—the right to pursue a business or profession free from arbitrary and excessive governmental interference—and included this basic right among the "privileges or immunities" of citizenship protected by the Fourteenth Amendment.

Subsequent history, however, has witnessed these clearly expressed intentions thwarted by the Supreme Court, with the result that the rights guaranteed by the privileges or immunities clause— especially economic liberty—are at best vulnerable or at worst routinely denied. What was designed as a mighty bulwark to shield individuals against government oppression has been utterly emasculated by judicial neglect, at great cost to all Americans but particularly to those outside the economic mainstream. A positive strategy for civil rights litigation should make as a top priority the restoration of the privileges or immunities of citizenship, including the fundamental individual right of economic liberty.

THE FOURTEENTH AMENDMENT
AND ECONOMIC LIBERTY

The era following the Civil War was permeated by the spirit of *laissez-faire*, with individual autonomy elevated to a moral absolute by the issue of slavery. Economic liberty was widely recognized as a vital component of individual autonomy. Declared William Lloyd Garrison, the leading anti-slavery theorist, "I avow myself to be a radical free trader, even to the extent of desiring the abolition of all custom-houses, as now constituted, throughout the world."[20] Placing the issue in the context of a human's rights, Herbert Spencer argued that

> [i]n putting a veto upon any commercial intercourse, or in putting obstacles in the way of any such intercourse, a government trenches upon men's liberties of action; and by so doing directly reverses its function. To secure for each man the fullest freedom to exercise his faculties compatible with the like freedom of all others, we find to be the State's duty. Now trade-prohibitions and trade-restrictions not only do not secure this freedom, they take it away. So that in enforcing them the State is transformed from a maintainer of rights into a violator of rights.[21]

But the dream of individual autonomy, though advanced by the Thirteenth Amendment's abolition of slavery, proved illusory. Before the Civil War had barely ended, southern legislators had already recognized that the surest way to frustrate the aims of emancipation was to destroy the economic liberty of the newly freed slaves. Determined to preserve the supply of cheap and plentiful labor and to maintain the status of blacks as a separate and subordinate caste, several southern states passed a series of laws called the "Black Codes." These laws placed severe restrictions on economic liberty, such as the right of blacks to freely bargain over terms and conditions of employment or to engage in certain trades or businesses.[22] Major General Carl Schurz, in his report to Congress on the condition of the South in 1865, observed that

> [t]he opposition to the negro's controlling his own labor, carrying on independently on his own account—in one word, working for his own benefit—showed itself in a variety of ways. Here and there municipal regulations were gotten up heavily taxing or otherwise impeding those trades and employments in which colored people are most likely to engage.[23]

These oppressions were foremost on the minds of the Reconstruction era lawmakers when they set about the task of framing the Civil Rights Act of 1866. Representative Martin Thayer explained that the proposed law was designed to protect the freedmen against

> laws which impair their ability to make contracts for labor in such manner as virtually to deprive them of the power of making such contracts. . . . I ask . . . what kind of freedom is that by which the man placed in a state of freedom is subject to the tyranny of laws which deprive him of rights which the humblest citizen in every State in Christendom enjoys . . . [such as] the liberty to engage in the ordinary pursuits of life?[24]

The resulting legislation cured these injustices by establishing that all citizens

> have the same right [to] make and enforce contracts, to sue, be parties, and give evidence, to inherit, purchase, lease, sell, hold, and convey real and personal property, and to full and equal benefit of all laws [for] the security of persons and property, as is enjoyed by white citizens, and shall be subject to like punishment, [and] to none other, any law . . . to the contrary notwithstanding.[25]

One of the bill's primary objects was to secure basic economic liberty. Representative William Lawrence argued that

> [i]t is idle to say that a citizen shall have the right to life, yet to deny him the right to labor, whereby alone he can live. It is a mockery to say that a citizen may have a right to live, and yet deny him the right to make a contract to secure the privilege and rewards of labor.[26]

Accordingly, the law was aimed at both methods by which "a State may undertake to deprive citizens of these absolute, inherent, and inalienable rights: either by prohibitory laws, or by a failure to protect any one of them."[27] Representative Lawrence made clear that the economic liberty protected against state interference was a universal liberty and was not restricted to the freed slaves: "This bill," he declared, "is not made for any class or creed, or race or color, but in the great future that awaits us will, if it become a law, protect every citizen."[28]

This law defining and establishing federal protection for basic civil rights, however, constituted a direct assault on traditional notions of the respective roles of the state and national governments with regard to civil rights. Before the Civil Rights Act of 1866, civil rights were largely entrusted to the states for protection.[29] But as Herman Belz recounts, the events following the Civil War quickly made it "apparent that the vindication of ordinary civil rights for blacks would require extraordinary efforts by the federal government."[30]

These efforts produced an immediate clash between Congress and President Andrew Johnson, who vetoed the bill on the grounds that Congress was without power to enact it. Though Congress passed the law over Johnson's veto, it moved at once to safeguard its provisions by "constitutionalizing" them in the form of a constitutional amendment. The first section of the subsequent Fourteenth Amendment provided that

> [n]o State shall make or enforce any law which shall abridge the privileges or immunities of citizens of the United States; nor shall any State deprive any person of life, liberty, or property, without due process of law; nor deny to any person within its jurisdiction the equal protection of the laws.

As Representative Lawrence later recounted, the amendment was necessary precisely because "civil rights were unsafe when left to the States where the evil of slavery still lived."[31] Thus, in enacting the Fourteenth Amendment, as Belz explains, Congress intended "unequivocally to transfer legislative power over civil rights from the states to the federal government, thus revolutionizing federal-state relations."[32] While Representative Bingham's first draft of the amendment merely extended to Congress the power to enforce the rights enumerated, he subsequently revised it as a self-executing declaration of rights and restraints on the power of states.[33]

As for the content of the rights embodied in the section, Belz notes, the amendment's framers "viewed the trilogy of privileges and immunities, due process, and equal protection of the laws as a caption for the rights enumerated in the Civil Rights Act [of 1866]."[34] As with the earlier law, the framers of the Fourteenth Amendment were motivated in large part by the desire to protect economic liberty. Senator Arthur Boreman complained, for instance, that the freedmen "have not been allowed in peace or security to pursue a trade or calling which they might have embarked in, or agricultural or professional pursuits, or otherwise."[35]

The amendment's framers considered such economic liberties as among the "privileges or immunities of citizens of the United States" protected by the amendment. The privileges or immunities clause was modeled after Article IV, section 2, of the original Constitution, which provides that "[t]he citizens of each State shall be entitled to all the privileges and immunities of citizens in the several States." The substance of these privileges and immunities were summarized by Justice Bushrod Washington in the 1823 case of *Corfield* v. *Coryell*, defining privileges and immunities to consist of those "which are, in their nature, fundamental; which belong, of right, to the citizens of all free governments." These rights included, among others, "the enjoyment of life and liberty, with the right to acquire and possess property of every kind, and to pursue and obtain happiness and safety, subject, nevertheless, to such restraints as the government may justly prescribe for the general good of the whole."[36]

However, this provision of the original Constitution placed only a partial limitation on the power of states to abridge such privileges and immunities, for it was held to require states only to protect such rights of citizens of *other* states to the same extent they protect such rights of their *own* citizens. Thus, while the Fourteenth Amendment did not alter the *substantive* rights that were included among the privileges and immunities of citizenship, the amendment's framers intended to effect a profound change in the extent to which states were obliged to respect those rights.

This point was made emphatically, time and again, by the amendment's framers. Senator Frederick Frelinghuysen underscored this fundamental change in a congressional debate in 1874. "The fourteenth amendment goes much further than the old Constitution," he declared. "It makes United States citizenship primary, and State citizenship derivative."[37] Quoting a decision by Justice Joseph Bradley, Senator Frelinghuysen explained that

> The "privileges and immunities" secured by the original Constitution were only such as each State gave to its own citizens. Each was prohibited from discriminating in favor of its own citizens and against the citizens of other States. But the fourteenth amendment prohibits the State from abridging the privileges and immunities of the citizens of the United States, whether its own citizens or any others. It not merely requires equality of privileges, but it demands that the privileges and immunities of all citizens shall be absolutely unabridged, unimpaired.[38]

Senator Jacob Howard sounded a similar theme eight years earlier. Under Article IV, section 2, of the original Constitution and the Bill of Rights, Howard observed, "the States are not restrained from violating the principles embraced in them except by their own local constitutions." As a consequence, Howard declared, the "great object of [the Fourteenth] amendment is . . . to restrain the power of the States and compel them at all times to respect these great fundamental guarantees."[39]

Thus, unlike the protections afforded by Article IV, section 2, the Fourteenth Amendment was designed to protect the rights of individuals against *their own* state governments. As Senator Boreman affirmed, the amendment "extends to every 'person,' whether he has come from another State or not."[40] To allow the states to retain largely unrestrained authority with respect to civil rights, the framers recognized, would render those civil rights a nullity.

In terms of the substantive content of the privileges or immunities embodied in the amendment, the framers of the Fourteenth Amendment shared a clear and common understanding; they discussed the nature of these rights at some length. In essence, they intended the amendment to incorporate natural rights, as set forth by Kent and Blackstone as well as by Justice Washington's restatement of those rights in *Corfield* v. *Coryell*.[41] Senator John Sherman viewed the privileges or immunities clause not only as applying the restraints of the original Constitution and Bill of Rights to the states, but as protecting the common law rights of individuals as well. Declared Sherman,

> What are those privileges and immunities? Are they only those defined in the Constitution, the rights secured by the [Bill of Rights]? Not at all. The great fountainhead, the great reservoir of the rights of an American citizen is the common law. . . . What are those rights? Sir, they are as innumerable as the sands of the sea.[42]

Senator Sherman viewed the rights embodied in the clause as self-executing, with the task of protecting those rights entrusted to the judiciary with natural law as its touchstone:

> That right must be determined from time to time by the judicial tribunals, and in determining it they will look first at the Constitution of the United States as the primary fountain of authority. If that does not define the right they will look for the unenumerated powers to the Declaration of American Independence, . . . [and] to the common law of England. . . . There they will find the fountain and reservoir of the rights of American[s].[43]

The amendment's architects clearly intended to protect economic liberty among the privileges or immunities of citizenship. Representative John A. Bingham, author of the first section of the Fourteenth Amendment, included within its scope "the liberty . . . to work in an honest calling and contribute by your toil in some sort to yourself, to the support of your fellowmen, and to be secure in the enjoyment of the fruits of your toil."[44] Senator William T. Hamilton expanded upon this broad theme, declaring that

> If there is a right that is natural and that belongs to me because I am a citizen and entitled to the protection of the laws, it is to transact my own private business in my own way without the interference of government. . . . [H]as not every person a right, to carry on his own occupation, to secure the fruits of his own industry . . . as long as it is

a legitimate exercise of this right and not vicious in itself, or against public policy, or against the natural rights of others?[45]

Likewise, Senator Matthew H. Carpenter noted that it was only the existence of the Fourteenth Amendment that "opened the bar to colored men," stating more generally that the privileges or immunities clause

> offers all the pursuits and avocations of life to the colored man in all the States of the Union. Strike down that amendment, or, what would be the same thing, construe it in such a niggardly spirit as to make it mean no more than the old Constitution meant, and you strike down the rights of the colored people all over this country. ...[46]

Senator Carpenter's fears, of course, proved prophetic: the Supreme Court did construe the Fourteenth Amendment in a narrow manner, purging the privileges or immunities clause of its rich content, to the particular detriment of the most disadvantaged in our society. As Joseph Tussman and Jacobus tenBroek have noted, "the purposes of these framers received short shrift at the hands of the Supreme Court.... The privileges and immunities clause was officially killed in the *Slaughter-House Cases*."[47] That decision markets a dismal chapter in the history of American constitutional jurisprudence, and one that we must overcome if we are to fulfill the great promise of civil rights.*

THE SLAUGHTER-HOUSE CASES

April 14, 1873, was a dark day for civil rights in America, for on that day the U.S. Supreme Court extinguished one of the most precious liberties of its citizens.

This nullification of individual liberty took place in an unusual context. In March 1869, the Louisiana legislature enacted a statute granting an exclusive 25-year slaughterhouse monopoly within New Orleans and other parishes, and ordering the closing of other existing slaughterhouses. The law also restricted the locations in which cattle could be landed and slaughtered, and established fees and an inspection process for such services.[48]

---

*For a contrary view that *Slaughter-House* represents a "narrow victory for judicial moderation," see Robert H. Bork, *The Tempting of America* (New York: Free Press, 1990), pp. 37–39. Bork also differs on the scope of the privileges or immunities clause, *id.,* pp. 180–182.

Though the law served some valid health objectives, historian Charles Lofgren recounts that "legislative bribery had greased passage of the law, with its most immediate beneficiaries—the seventeen participants in the corporation it established—adroitly distributing shares of stock and cash."[49] The slaughterhouse monopoly thus served the private interests of those who agitated for its passage, to the detriment of those who were subsequently excluded.

The Supreme Court case consolidated three lawsuits: one by a butchers' association to enjoin enforcement of the law, the second by the Louisiana Attorney General on behalf of the holder of the monopoly to enjoin an attempt by stockdealers and butchers to acquire a tract of property to land and slaughter cattle, and the third by the monopoly corporation to enjoin its competitors.[50] The juxtaposition of these parties suggests that whatever the purported purpose of the law, the parties were fighting about the right to compete versus the power to restrain such competition.

The butchers argued that the slaughterhouse monopoly imposed an involuntary servitude under the Thirteenth Amendment since it compelled them to pay the monopolist for the right to carry on their own businesses. They also argued that it violated the Fourteenth Amendment's guarantees of privileges or immunities of citizenship, equal protection, and due process.[51] The parties did not press vigorously the arguments on the second two clauses,[52] thus focusing the dispute on the scope of the privileges or immunities clause.

A bitterly divided Court upheld the law in its entirety by a 5–4 vote. The majority decision was authored by Justice Samuel F. Miller; the three dissenting opinions were written by Justice Stephen Field (joined by Chief Justice Salmon Chase, Justice Noah H. Swayne, and Justice Joseph P. Bradley), Justice Bradley (joined by Justice Swayne), and Justice Swayne.

Going much further than was necessary to sustain the law, the majority opinion, as Michael Kent Curtis observes, applied the Fourteenth Amendment's protections "so narrowly that the privileges or immunities clause was virtually read out of the Constitution.[53] Professor Edward Corwin remarks that "[u]nique among constitutional provisions, the privileges and immunities clause of the Fourteenth Amendment enjoys the distinction of having been rendered a 'practical nullity' by a single decision of the Supreme Court rendered within five years after its ratification."[54]

To reach such a result, Justice Miller had to engage in some creative reconstruction of recent history. He began by noting correctly that "the one pervading purpose" of the Civil War–era constitutional amendments was to ensure "freedom of the slave race." While acknowledging that the protections extended to others as well, Miller viewed the necessity of protecting the rights of the freedmen as "the pervading spirit" of the enactments.[55] Miller noted, for instance, that the affirmation of Negro "citizenship" was designed to overturn the pre–Civil War *Dred Scott* decision[56] in which the Supreme Court held that blacks could not be citizens within the meaning of the Constitution.[57]

Having set the stage for a narrow construction of the amendment by focusing on its immediate objectives rather than its universal application, Justice Miller proceeded to set forth an interpretive construct that would allow him to emasculate the amendment's substantive protections. Miller divided the rights of citizenship into two classes: the rights of national citizenship, i.e., those that "owe their existence to the Federal government, its national character, its Constitution, or its laws"; and the broader category of general civil rights, within which the economic liberty rights asserted by the butchers were included.[58]

The first category, the rights of national citizenship, was narrowly defined to include only those rights explicitly specified by federal law, such as the right of access to the operations of foreign commerce, the right to move freely from state to state and enjoy the same rights as citizens of those states, the right of *habeas corpus*, the right of access to navigable waters within the United States, the right of freedom of assembly, and the clearly identified substantive provisions of the recent amendments.[59]

The second category, according to Justice Miller, included the broad array of "privileges and immunities" of citizenship as set forth by Justice Washington in *Corfield* v. *Coryell*.[60] This broader domain of civil rights, Justice Miller correctly observed, was one "heretofore belonging exclusively to the States."[61] Hence the question before the Court, as Miller defined it, was whether it was

> the purpose of the fourteenth amendment, by the simple declaration that no State should make or enforce any law which shall abridge the privileges and immunities of citizens of the United States, to transfer the security and protection of all the civil rights which we have mentioned, from the States to the Federal government?[62]

Though even a cursory reading of the legislative history of the Fourteenth Amendment would have yielded an emphatic and unequivocal affirmative response—indeed, the amendment's architects stressed time and again that it was their intent to protect basic civil rights against infringement by the states and to define those rights broadly—Justice Miller concluded otherwise. Miller contended that the privileges or immunities clause of the Fourteenth Amendment only slightly expanded the reach of Article IV, section 2, of the original Constitution, whose "sole purpose was to declare to the several States, that whatever those rights, as you grant or establish them to your own citizens . . ., the same, neither more nor less, shall be the measure of the rights of citizens of other States within your jurisdiction."[63] The Fourteenth Amendment's only innovation in this respect, Miller declared, was to extend protection against infringement by state governments to those few substantive rights that derived from United States citizenship. Though conceding that the rights asserted by the butchers were within the meaning of the term "privileges and immunities," Miller concluded they were among those "which belong to citizens of the States as such, and . . . [are not] placed under the special care of the Federal government."[64]

In so ruling, the *Slaughter-House* majority engaged in severely flawed reasoning. The Court's central error was in its perpetuation of the distinction between civil rights arising from the respective spheres of national and state citizenship, a distinction the amendment's framers intended to eliminate. As Belz explains, Justice Miller departed from legislative intent "by treating national and state aspects [of citizenship] as separate and exclusive rather than complementary and concentric."[65]

Hence, even though the Court acknowledged that the primary objective of the amendment was to protect the "slave race," it interpreted the amendment as not encompassing the very right that was most brazenly denied to blacks—economic liberty. As Michael Kent Curtis observes, "why an amendment, which Miller incorrectly thought was designed only to protect blacks, would focus on things such as traveling back and forth to Washington, D.C., and to the seaports and protection on high seas and in foreign countries, Justice Miller did not explain."[66] Indeed, it is absurd to conclude, as did the *Slaughter-House* majority, that the framers of the amendment would worry about these incidental rights, but not basic civil rights such as freedom to contract over the terms of labor or to engage in a chosen business or profession. Such a notion is repudiated not only by reason but by the amendment's legislative history.

Indeed, the Court's "strange reading of the language of the Fourteenth Amendment,"[67] charges Curtis, was attributable to the fact that "the history of abuses that led to the amendment received superficial and cursory attention at best," and the legislative history "received no attention at all."[68] As a consequence of this departure from the framers' intent, Curtis notes, "the most basic civil liberties were to be protected only by state laws and state constitutions. In this respect the situation was much like it had been before the Civil War."[69]

The dissenters vigorously and eloquently defended the spirit of the privileges or immunities clause against the majority's onslaught. Justice Stephen Field, writing for four justices, set forth the applicable constitutional framework, derived from the natural rights construct in which fundamental rights are paramount, but in which the popular will is allowed freely to manifest itself in matters not unduly interfering with such rights.

Since the *Slaughter-House Cases* presented an asserted "police power" regulation, the dissenters were appropriately deferential. The police power, wrote Justice Field, "undoubtedly extends to all regulations affecting the health, good order, morals, peace and safety of society"; and "when these are not in conflict with any constitutional prohibitions, or fundamental principles, they cannot be successfully assailed in a judicial tribunal." However, this police power was limited, Field declared, for "under the pretense of prescribing a police regulation the State cannot be permitted to encroach upon any of the just rights of the citizen, which the Constitution intended to secure against abridgment."[70] The judiciary's task, then, was to look behind the asserted rationale to determine whether the regulation was a proper exercise of the police power or a mere pretext.

Justice Field proceeded to analyze the Louisiana enactments in the context of these two categories. He had no difficulty in concluding that the cattle landing and inspection requirements were proper police regulations. He likewise stated that grants of monopolies were permissible for "franchises of a public character," such as roads, bridges, and so forth. But such a public franchise, Field reasoned, "is a very different thing from a grant, with exclusive privileges, of a right to pursue one of the ordinary trades or callings of life, which is a right appertaining solely to the individual."[71]

This distinction made, Justice Field framed the broader legal issue before the Court as "nothing less than whether the recent Amendments to the Federal Constitution protect the citizens of the United States against the deprivation of their common rights by state legislation."[72] Unlike the majority, Field concluded in the affirmative. The Fourteenth Amendment, the dissenters recounted, "was adopted to obviate objections which had been raised and pressed with great force to the validity of the [1866] Civil Rights Act, and to place the common rights of the American citizens under the protection of the National government."[73]

In terms of substantive protections, Field stated, the Fourteenth Amendment "does not attempt to confer any new privileges or immunities upon citizens, or to enumerate or define those already existing. It assumes there are such privileges and immunities which belong of right to citizens as such, and ordains that they shall not be abridged by State legislation."[74] Field then assailed the logical underpinnings of the majority's holding:

> If this inhibition has no reference to privileges and immunities of this character, ... it was a vain and idle enactment, which accomplished nothing, and most unnecessarily excited Congress and the people on

its passage. With privileges and immunities thus designated no State could ever have interfered by its laws, and no new constitutional provision was required to inhibit such interference. ... But if the Amendment refers to the natural and inalienable rights which belong to all citizens, the inhibition has a profound significance and consequence.[75]

The correct constitutional rule, Field concluded, is that the "privileges and immunities of the citizens of the United States, of every one of them, is secured against abridgment in any form by any State."[76]

Turning to the specific regulations, Field found that "[a]ll monopolies in any known trade are an invasion of these privileges, for they encroach upon the liberty of citizens to acquire property and pursue happiness,"[77] rights denominated as privileges and immunities of citizenship by Justice Washington in *Corfield* v. *Coryell* and as civil rights by the 1866 Civil Rights Act.[78] Tracing the liberty to its origins, Field noted that the common law "condemned all monopolies in any known trade or manufacture, and declared void all grants of special privileges whereby others could be ... hindered in their lawful trade." The "main ground" of the common law rule on monopolies "was their interference with the liberty of the subject to pursue for his maintenance and that of his family any lawful trade or employment. This liberty is assumed to be the natural right of every Englishman."[79]

Justice Field concluded that such liberty could properly be restrained or regulated only by "just, equal, and impartial laws."[80] The slaughterhouse monopoly, he charged, was not such a law. "[I]t is to me a matter of profound regret that its validity is recognized by a majority of this court," Field lamented, "for by it the right of free labor, one of the most sacred and imprescriptible rights of man, is violated."[81]

Justice Joseph P. Bradley, writing for himself and for Justice Noah H. Swayne, expanded upon Justice Field's views, placing more sharply into focus the appropriate mode of judicial analysis. Like Justice Field, Bradley articulated a deferential standard of judicial review:

The right of a state to regulate the conduct of its citizens is undoubtedly a very broad and extensive one, and not to be lightly restricted. But there are certain fundamental rights which this right of regulation cannot infringe. It may prescribe the manner of their exercise, but it cannot subvert the rights themselves.[82]

The legislative scheme before the Court, Justice Bradley explained, triggered a two-part inquiry. First, "[i]s it one of the rights and privileges of a citizen of the United States to pursue such civil employment as he may choose to adopt, subject to such reasonable regulations as may be prescribed by law?" If so, the Court should proceed to determine whether the enactment at issue is "a reasonable regulation of that employment which the legislature has a right to impose[.]"[83]

Tracing the right of economic liberty to common law, the Declaration of Independence, and *Corfield* v. *Coryell*,[84] Justice Bradley concluded that the first part of the inquiry was satisfied:

For the preservation, exercise, and enjoyment of [his] rights the individual citizen, as a necessity, must be free to adopt such calling, profession, or trade as may seem to him most conducive. . . . Without this right he cannot be a freeman. This right to choose one's calling is an essential part of that liberty which it is the object of government to protect; and a calling, when chosen, is a man's property and right. Liberty and property are not protected where these rights are arbitrarily assailed.[85]

Having found that the regulations constrained the exercise of a fundamental right, Justice Bradley proceeded to determine whether they were reasonable. The statute's restriction of locations for slaughterhouses and creation of inspection standards were "clearly a police regulation," Bradley found. But "[t]o compel a butcher . . . to slaughter [his] cattle in another person's slaughterhouse and to pay him a toll therefor," Bradley declared, "is such a restriction upon the trade as materially to interfere with its prosecution." Such a monopoly, Bradley concluded, is invalid as "one of those arbitrary and unjust laws made in the interest of a few scheming individuals."[86]

Justice Swayne, dissenting separately, placed the Fourteenth Amendment in its historical and political context and assailed the majority for subverting the clear intent of the amendment's framers.

"By the Constitution, as it stood before the [Civil] war," Justice Swayne recounted, "ample protection was given against oppression by the Union, but little was given against wrong and oppression by the States. That want was intended to be supplied by this amendment."[87] The first eleven amendments to the Constitution "were intended to be checks and limitations upon the government which that instrument called into existence,"[88] Swayne explained. But "the light of experience" revealed to the public mind that "there was less danger of tyranny in the head than of anarchy and tyranny in the members."[89]

As a consequence of this experience, Congress adopted the Civil War amendments, which "are a new departure, and mark an important epoch in the constitutional history of the country," Swayne remarked, for they "trench directly upon the power of the States, and deeply affect those bodies." Thus understood, Swayne declared, "these amendments may be said to rise to the dignity of a new Magna Charta."[90]

Despite the substantial change marked by the amendments, Swayne observed, the provisions "are all eminently conservative in their character," and are "necessary to enable the government of the nation to secure to every one within its jurisdiction the rights and privileges enumerated, which, according to the plainest considerations of reason and justice and the fundamental principles of the social compact, all are entitled to enjoy."[91]

Proclaiming that "[o]ur duty is to execute the law, not make it," Justice Swayne protested that the majority's opinion "defeats, by a limitation not anticipated, the intent of those by whom the amendment was framed."[92] Swayne concluded by voicing the "hope that the consequences to follow may prove less serious and far-reaching than the minority fear they will be."[93]

THE AFTERMATH OF *SLAUGHTER-HOUSE*

The *Slaughter-House* decision outraged the architects of the amendment so recently passed. A number of Republicans denied the authority of the decision.[94] Condemning the Court for its holding that the amendment protected only those rights derived from national citizenship and comparing *Slaughter-House* to the earlier *Dred Scott* ruling, Senator Timothy Howe proclaimed "what the American people and I believe the civilized world have already said of another ... decision of that same court, that it is not law and cannot be law."[95] Political scientist John W. Burgess charged that *Slaughter-House* repudiated the "great gain in the domain of civil liberty won by the terrible exertion of the nation by appeal to arms. I have perfect confidence that the day will come when it will be seen to be intensely reactionary and will be overruled."[96]

Just as their handiwork was being undone by the Supreme Court, however, the ability of the congressional champions of civil rights to do much about it was diminishing. The abolitionist leaders were aging and dying off, the Grant administration was paralyzed by scandals, the Democrats captured Congress for the first time in 1874, and the post-war pressure for reform waned as the country turned its attention to other issues.[97]

Thus *Slaughter-House* was allowed to stand, and its consequences were predictable and immediate. From the outset, the Supreme Court applied *Slaughter-House* to uphold other deprivations of economic liberty, including an Illinois law forbidding qualified women from practicing law.[98]

Ironically, the greatest initial impact was not in the area of economic liberty, but in public accommodations. Republicans in Congress were attempting to pass a new civil rights law guaranteeing equal opportunity in schools and public accommodations. But as Alfred Avins notes, Democratic opponents "eagerly seized upon the recently-decided *Slaughter-House Cases* ... to point out the difference between the privileges of national citizenship and the privileges of state citizenship."[99] The Democrats successfully struck school desegregation provisions of the Civil Rights Act of 1875[100] by arguing that Congress had no remedial authority except with respect to the privileges or immunities of national citizenship. Hence, *Slaughter-House* provided the foundation for the imposition by state governments of "separate but equal" a full quarter century before *Plessy* v. *Ferguson*!

Nor did it take much time for the southern legislatures to exhume the Black Codes in a slightly more sophisticated, yet no less oppressive, version. *Slaughter-House* unleashed the state governments to enact "Jim Crow" laws, many of which consisted of ostensibly race-neutral regulations of labor contracts and entry into trades and professions that had the effect of severely restricting economic opportunities for blacks.[101] Later laws, such as the federal Davis-Bacon Act, were aimed at restricting competition from black labor although they were cast in a benevolent veneer.

During the late 19th and early 20th centuries, the Supreme Court acted for a time to protect economic liberty against arbitrary or excessive government regulations. In *Yick Wo* v. *Hopkins*,[102] an 1886 decision that remains good law, the Court invalidated on equal protection grounds a San Francisco ordinance that limited laundry establishments to those constructed of brick or stone, which was a thinly disguised attempt to drive out Chinese entrepreneurs. Highlighting the precious nexus between economic liberty and individual freedom, the Court declared that

> in our system, while sovereign powers are delegated to the agencies of government, sovereignty itself remains with the people, by whom and for whom all government exists and acts. . . . [T]he very idea that one man may be compelled to hold his life, or the means of living, or any material right essential to the enjoyment of life, at the mere will of another, seems to be intolerable in any country where freedom prevails, as being the essence of slavery itself.[103]

Most of the economic liberty decisions of this period were decided on "substantive due process" grounds—a theory that gives substantive protection to the liberty and property interests protected by the due process clause. This theory was exemplified by the 1905 *Lochner* v. *New York* decision,[104] in which the Court struck down as a violation of liberty of contract a statute limiting employment in bakeries to 10 hours per day and 60 hours per week.

Writing for the majority, Justice Rufus Peckham found that the "right to purchase or to sell labor is part of the liberty protected by th[e Fourteenth] amendment, unless there are circumstances which exclude the right."[105] The Court rejected the state's public health and safety rationale,[106] sounding a remarkably prophetic warning that

> there is a limit to the valid exercise of the police power by the State. . . .

Otherwise the Fourteenth Amendment would have no efficacy and the legislatures of the States would have unbounded power, and it would be enough to say that any piece of legislation was enacted to conserve the morals, the health, or the safety of the people; such legislation would be valid, no matter how absolutely without foundation the claim might be.[107]

In a discussion that could just as easily describe the current state of economic regulation, the Court observed that "many of the laws of this character, while passed under what is claimed to be the police power for the purpose of protecting the public health or welfare, are, in reality, passed from other motives."[108] If the judiciary failed to safeguard the individual against such abuses, the majority reasoned, "[n]o trade, no occupation, no mode of earning one's living, could escape this all-pervading power, . . . although such limitation might seriously cripple the ability of the laborer to support himself and his family."[109]

In dissent, Justice Holmes cavalierly dismissed such prescient concerns as mere ideological claptrap. Holmes declared that "[t]his case is decided upon an economic theory which a large part of the country does not entertain," namely, the "shibboleth" of "[t]he liberty of the citizen to do as he likes so long as he does not interfere with the liberty of others to do the same." Proclaiming that "a constitution is not intended to embody a particular economic theory,"[110] Holmes sounded the death knell for economic liberty.

Holmes' dissent exposed the tenuous intellectual underpinnings of substantive due process and proved a harbinger of the judicial abdication to follow. As James Dorn explains,

> While the Court had a number of general insights and principles to inform its constitutional jurisprudence, it had nothing like a well-developed theory of rights or theory of constitutional interpretation in which it could place its confidence. Absent this confidence, and under political pressure to bend to the will of the majority, the Court eventually yielded its role to the political branches. Thereafter, at least in the area of property rights and economic liberties, the legislature rather than the Court would be the principal interpreter of the Constitution. Our property rights and economic liberties would be

determined by political will rather than by the moral reasoning that stood behind the Constitution.[111]

Holmes's desire to craft a constitutional imprimatur for economic authoritarianism was ultimately accomplished by the New Deal Court in *West Coast Hotel Co.* v. *Parrish*.[112] By a 5–4 decision, the Court upheld a Washington state law establishing a minimum wage for women and minors, overruling a previous decision that struck down a minimum wage law pursuant to the *Lochner* doctrine.[113] Rather than measuring the necessity of the regulation against the extent of its restraint on liberty, the Court assumed the statute's constitutionality and overlooked its effect on fundamental rights. Declaring that the "Constitution does not speak of freedom of contract,"[114] Chief Justice Charles Evans Hughes adopted a remarkably paternalistic approach. Hughes rejected out of hand the "point that has been strongly stressed that adult employees should be deemed competent to make their own contracts," assuming instead an "inequality in the footing of the parties."[115] After all, Hughes explained, the contracting parties were women, "in whose protection the State has a special interest" justified by the "woman's physical structure and the performance of maternal functions"[116] and by their "unequal position with respect to bargaining power" that renders them "defenseless against the denial of a living wage."[117] Displaying a noteworthy ignorance of basic economics, the Chief Justice concluded that without a minimum wage, the women could find themselves on relief. This, the majority concluded, would amount to "a subsidy for unconscionable employers. The community may direct its law-making power to correct the abuse which springs from their selfish disregard of the public interest."[118]

In an eloquent dissent, Justice George Sutherland assailed the majority's casual disregard of precedent. "It is urged that the question involved should now receive fresh consideration ... because of 'the economic conditions which have supervened,'" remarked Sutherland, "but the meaning of the Constitution does not change with the ebb and flow of economic events."[119] Rejecting the majority's shameless paternalism, Sutherland took the more enlightened view that "[t]he ability to make a fair bargain ... does not depend on [a person's] sex."[120] Under the doctrine abandoned by the majority, Sutherland explained, the Court had never ruled that freedom of contract was absolute, but rather that "freedom of contract was the general rule and restraint the exception; and that the power to abridge that freedom could only be justified by the existence of exceptional circumstances."[121]

This equation was reversed by the Court majority, never to be reconsidered in the context of economic liberty. As Norman Karlin has observed, the legacy of *West Coast Hotel* is "pure majoritarianism; precisely what Madison and other Framers feared most. The legislature was now able to roam at will and proceed without restraint."[122]

Indeed, the Supreme Court has seemingly carved out for economic liberty a unique analytical category; alone among the civil rights of Americans, governments may compromise it with impunity, subject to no meaningful judicial review. The Court admitted as much in its 1976 decision in *City of New Orleans* v. *Dukes*,[123] in which it unanimously upheld a municipal ordinance that limited to two the number of vendor pushcarts permitted in the French Quarter and which destroyed the plaintiff's livelihood. Though the Court of Appeals found the prohibition totally arbitrary and irrational, the Supreme Court reversed and held that "in the local economic sphere, it is only the invidious discrimination, the wholly arbitrary act, which cannot stand consistently with the Fourteenth Amendment." The Supreme Court acknowledged that "this Court consistently defers to legislative determinations as to the desirability of particular statutory determinations."[124]

The mode of analysis the Court purports to apply to regulations that have an impact on economic liberty is called "rational basis," but in reality it typically amounts to no scrutiny at all. As Norman Karlin observes, such scrutiny consists of two questions:

> (1) Does the legislation involve a legitimate state purpose? The answer, of course, is always "yes"; (2) Do the implementing means, *as a theoretical matter only*, rationally relate to the legitimate purpose? Here, too, the answer is always "yes."[125]

"At this point," notes Karlin, "judicial inquiry end[s]."[126]

As Leonard Levy wryly observes, "[i]f Nancy Dukes [the hotdog pushcart vendor in the French Quarter] had been a 'nude dancer ..., she might have pleaded freedom of expression under the first amendment." But "selling hot dogs is just commerce, and therefore entitled to little constitutional respect, even if it involves one's livelihood."[127] Levy notes that in the past half-century, the Supreme Court has virtually never struck down economic regulation.[128]

The real-world consequences of this wholesale judicial abdication are devastating. In such areas as professional licensing and government-conferred business monopolies, traditional avenues for entry into the marketplace and for upward mobility are all but curtailed. Such laws are ubiquitous: California alone requires licenses for entry into 178 occupations. Levy remarks that "[a]bout the only people who are unlicensed in California are clergymen and university professors, apparently because no one takes them seriously."[129] Likewise, government-enforced taxicab monopolies exist in virtually every major city, creating arbitrary barriers to entry into the taxicab business, just as the anti-jitney law prevents Alfredo Santos from offering that transportation option to Houston residents.

Many of these laws have only the most attenuated connection to legitimate public health or safety concerns; they are intended instead to insulate those engaged in the trade or business from competition. Indeed, many of the standards are determined and enforced by the regulated industries themselves, who have an incentive to minimize competition.[130]

These laws are an enduring and debilitating relic of the Jim Crow era. Though only a few trace their origins to overt discriminatory intent, they are typically designed to exclude outsiders. As Dr. Walter Williams remarks, "The[se] laws are not discriminatory in the sense that they are aimed specifically at blacks. But they are discriminatory in the sense that they deny full opportunity for the most disadvantaged Americans, among whom blacks are disproportionately represented."*[131]

---

*Some commentators have criticized *Changing Course* for what they perceive is a suggestion that laws that arbitrarily restrict entrepreneurial opportunities are violations of civil rights because they have an adverse impact on blacks and other minorities. Though they do have such an effect, laws that arbitrarily restrict entrepreneurial opportunities are not violations of civil rights because the people affected are blacks, rather they are violations of civil rights because the people affected are Americans.

Specific examples abound. Were it not for excessive government regulation, the taxicab business, with relatively low start-up costs, offers fairly easy entry to aspiring entrepreneurs. In Washington, D.C., which has fairly open entry and modest licensing fees, the overwhelming majority of cabs are owned by independent, minority owner-operators. Conversely, the New York City taxicab monopoly precludes such opportunities for economic outsiders. Artificial restraints on supply—the City has issued no new "medallions" since World War II—has driven the price of the permits to more than $100,000. Likewise, in cities where entry is restricted by a public utilities commission, the entrenched incumbents typically dominate the commission to exclude competition.[132]

Similarly, occupational licensing regulations that exceed those requirements that are necessary to protect public health and safety often present an insurmountable obstacle to people outside the economic mainstream. Stuart Dorsey reports, for instance, that licensing in Missouri for beauticians and cosmetologists requires applicants not only to demonstrate competency through a "hands-on" practical examination, but also to pass a difficult written test that includes questions on such esoteric concerns as the chemical composition of bones. Not surprisingly, black candidates have passed the *performance* portion of the examination at the same rate as whites, but the written examination excludes blacks at a vastly disproportionate rate from engaging in the profession for which they are otherwise demonstrably qualified.[133]

The aggregate exclusionary effects of such occupational licensing laws—many of which apply to occupations in which the need to protect the public is minimal—are substantial, since fully 10 percent of the workforce is employed in licensed occupations.[134] The secondary consequences of such restraints go almost without saying: if traditional avenues for earning a share of the American dream are foreclosed, other means of survival—welfare dependency, illicit activities, quotas—will increase.

The framers of the Fourteenth Amendment recognized that the use of the coercive apparatus of the state to deny economic self-determination constitutes a serious denial of civil rights. As Levy argues, "Making a living is fundamental to one's personhood and stake in society."[135]

Economic liberty is essential to individual empowerment, and the abdication by the judicial branch of its constitutional obligation to protect civil rights is one of the great failures of American jurisprudence. If our nation is to regain its status as a beacon of opportunity, we must begin by restoring economic liberty to its rightful place among our most precious civil rights.

DISMANTLING *SLAUGHTER-HOUSE*

As a long-range strategy, we should establish as our ultimate objective the reversal of the *Slaughter-House Cases*, much as the NAACP did when it set as its long-range goal the toppling of *Plessy* v. *Ferguson*. Such an effort will require the same tenacity, creativity, and commitment that were deployed by the NAACP and its allies.

Why *Slaughter-House*? Because just as *Plessy* v. *Ferguson* epitomized the denial of equality under law, so does *Slaughter-House* stand as a nullification of fundamental individual rights. The quest for civil rights is incomplete without such an effort.

Moreover, an emphasis on restoring the privileges or immunities clause to its intended meaning offers the greatest promise for protecting fundamental individual rights. Attempts to expand contemporary versions of substantive due process to once again encompass economic liberty are unlikely to succeed. As a threshold matter, substantive due process requires a more difficult argument. As Philip Kurland reminds us, "only the privileges or immunities clause speaks to matters of substance; certainly the language of due process and equal protection does not."[136]

Moreover, as Karlin warns, a "return to *Lochnerism*" is "the pejorative of all pejoratives."[137] The *Lochner* decision is one of the few jurisprudential issues on which many liberals and conservatives agree (though for different reasons), rendering that decision what Patrick Gudridge calls "a kind of 'anti-icon,' an infernal image of all that we must avoid in constitutional adjudication."[138] This widespread condemnation of *Lochner* is excessive, since the Court's primary error consisted of misidentifying the clause of the

Fourteenth Amendment that was intended to provide substantive protection to individual liberties, choosing to rely on the due process rather than the privileges or immunities clause. The Court also may have applied the substantive due process doctrine inconsistently, sometimes favoring business interests over minorities and women.[139]

Ample reason thus exists, on tactical as well as doctrinal grounds, to avoid attempts to exhume *Lochner*. In refraining from doing so, however, we should bear in mind that whatever the shortcomings of the *Lochner* doctrine, they pale in comparison to Justice Holmes' dissent, which Charles Fried aptly has characterized as "the source of our modern intellectual difficulties"[140] in this area of law. Though the Fourteenth Amendment's framers indeed may not have intended to provide substantive protection to individual rights through the due process clause, they clearly intended the amendment to provide such protection in some manner.

Meanwhile, efforts to protect property rights through a more vigorous application of the Constitution's "takings" clause,[141] though extremely promising and vitally important, do not necessarily cover the full range of substantive rights included within the meaning of privileges and immunities. Still, though they are not discussed here, property rights arguments are often compatible with the Fourteenth Amendment strategies discussed below and can be used in tandem by creative litigators.[142]

The privileges or immunities clause carries considerably less baggage than substantive due process and provides a sound constitutional vehicle with which to advance fundamental individual rights. Kurland predicts that in the future development of Fourteenth Amendment jurisprudence, "it will be the privileges or immunities clause, placed first among [the amendment's] grand restraints on government, that will be the center of attention."[143] The time for such an approach is ripe, Kurland argues:

> American society is rapidly moving toward the condition in which individual judgments and actions govern less and less of our behavior and formal and informal governments secure more and more power over individual activities. ... Lawsuits are now more and more concerned with the rights of classes, not individuals; of consumers, or

women, or blacks, or the aged, or the young. In short, we are on the road back from contract to status. . . . With government in control of so many essentials of our life, where in the Constitution can we turn for haven against the impositions of *1984*? . . . I expect it will come as an attempt to define the privileges or immunities of American citizenship.[144]

Another reason to pursue *Slaughter-House* is its inherent vulnerability. The case was wrongly decided. The majority opinion ignores clear legislative intent. Both the legal and practical arguments for overruling it are strong. That is not to suggest that toppling *Slaughter-House* will be easy; on the contrary, it has stood for well over a century, though that may be so in part because no significant attack has ever been mounted against it. But the weight of *stare decisis* will surely prove an impediment. On the other hand, the right case will have both the law and equity to commend it, just as *Brown* v. *Board of Education* did in its challenge to *Plessy*.

What are the likely effects of overturning *Slaughter-House*? First and foremost, it would mean far greater security for the forgotten civil rights—primarily economic liberty, which has singularly lacked judicial protection, but also all manner of private property rights, liberty of contract, and other incidents of personal autonomy. The general sphere of natural rights envisioned by the framers of the Fourteenth Amendment would, as Kurland asserts, provide a new bulwark for protecting individual liberty against the state.

In jurisprudential terms, reversing *Slaughter-House* would mean that in matters affecting the privileges or immunities of citizenship, the courts will no longer reflexively defer to legislative will. Instead, whenever the exercise of government power implicates one of the privileges or immunities of citizenship, it will trigger what Randy Barnett calls the "constitutional presumption in favor of individual liberty."[145]

Whatever the analysis is called—"rational basis," "intermediate scrutiny," or some other term—the courts should consider at least two factors in determining the constitutionality of the challenged governmental restraint. First, they should determine whether the law is designed to promote a legitimate public health, safety, or welfare objective. Second, they should assess whether the legislation actually serves the purported objectives. This inquiry may to some extent include a balancing of the magnitude of the harm against the importance of the public interest served. Such an inquiry would provide appropriate deference to the legislature, which is entrusted in the first instance with balancing competing interests. But judicial review is essential to prevent abuses of individual rights.

As an example, consider a challenge by an aspiring taxicab driver to New York City's taxicab medallion system. The city would defend the law on the grounds of consumer safety, traffic congestion, and so forth. A court properly applying the privileges or immunities clause would, as the first step in its inquiry, find that the law imposed an absolute restraint on the plaintiff's right to pursue his chosen lawful profession, which would make out a *prima facie* violation of the Fourteenth Amendment. The court would also find that the stated purposes of the law are legitimate police power objectives. But the court would proceed to consider whether the "means" employed to advance those objectives—an outright monopoly with no new permits granted since World War II—were unreasonably burdensome.

The court would likely conclude that while insurance and inspection requirements and possibly some regulations of minimum qualifications were lawful, the outright exclusion of newcomers excessively and unnecessarily burdened the plaintiff's privileges or immunities of citizenship. Such a decision would protect the legislature's ability to protect the public welfare while protecting basic individual freedoms.

The precise contours of this framework are, of course, uncertain. Indeed, the specific restrictions challenged in both *Slaughter-House* and *Lochner* would probably present close questions. But surely the type of arbitrary and oppressive restraint at issue in the *Dukes* case would fall. In the process, individuals would finally have somewhere to turn to protect their basic right to control their own destinies, fulfilling at last the aspirations of the architects of the Fourteenth Amendment.

Direct Assaults on Slaughter-House

Since *Slaughter-House* is a Supreme Court precedent, it will take a decision of the Supreme Court to squarely overturn it. Lower courts are unlikely to premise decisions protecting economic liberty (or other civil rights)* on the privileges or immunities clause. Hence, a direct assault on *Slaughter-House* may appear to start out as something other than that: aside from pleading a violation of the privileges or immunities clause in the complaint, the issue might not appear until the case reaches the Supreme Court.

Accordingly, the litigator in this endeavor must pursue two objectives at once. First, the case must be framed and argued using "mainstream" legal arguments like due process and equal protection, along perhaps with statutory "hooks" like the Sherman Act or Title VII. The reason for this approach is two-fold: it provides a realistic chance for the client to win, and it incrementally chips away at the *Slaughter-House* doctrine without doing so overtly. Each case provides a "building block" for economic liberty. Thus, even if *Slaughter-House* continues to stand, economic liberty will gain greater protection.

Simultaneously, the litigator must view every case as a candidate for eventually challenging *Slaughter-House*. In this regard, a loser is a winner, for only a case in which an adverse judgment is rendered allows the losing lawyer to frame the issues before the Supreme Court. Every case in which economic liberty is denied is a potential candidate to confront *Slaughter-House*, since that decision lurks behind every judicial abdication on questions of economic liberty.

Both facets of this strategy require excellent facts. Each case should present (1) an obviously arbitrary, oppressive, and/or anachronistic restraint on individual liberty; and (2) a sympathetic plaintiff. Economic liberty cases would typically involve a barrier to entry-level entrepreneurial opportunities, where the public interest served by the regulation is slight but the impact is severe. The basic principles derived from favorable holdings can provide a foundation for expanding the doctrine.

---

*The strategies discussed here are framed in terms of economic liberty but are applicable to other privileges or immunities as well.

In every such case that is presented for consideration to the Supreme Court, the litigator should include the issue of whether *Slaughter-House* should be overturned as one of the questions presented. This approach provides the Court with the opportunity to make either incremental changes—as it did before finally overturning *Plessy*—or to reverse *Slaughter-House* outright. Since we start essentially from ground zero, every victory, no matter how small, is an important triumph for economic liberty.

In the meantime, the groundwork for overturning *Slaughter-House* must be established both in legal scholarship and public opinion. Renewed scholarly interest in the privileges or immunities clause and more generally on the jurisprudence of economic liberty would provide an important foundation. Likewise, popular articles raising public consciousness on economic liberty as a new frontier in the battle for civil rights[146] will greatly assist in generating public support and in gaining a clear moral high ground. Such efforts may also have the salutary incidental effect of encouraging legislative reforms.

Slowly but surely, such efforts will erode the underpinnings of *Slaughter-House*, until the day on which the entire structure eventually collapses under its own oppressive weight.

Ancillary Tactics

As previously noted, until the privileges or immunities clause regains some of its lost vitality, challenges to vindicate the rights encompassed by that clause should initially focus on complementary, but potentially more immediately fruitful, legal theories such as the takings clause, due process, equal protection, and interstate commerce. The challenges should also focus on statutory protections such as antitrust and Title VII.

Due process and equal protection are especially promising, because the "means/ends" framework applied in some decisions is similar (though presently far less vigorous) to that suggested above in the context of the privileges or immunities clause.

Under equal protection analysis, though the "rational basis" test is applied, the courts will sometimes look behind a legislative classification if it singles out a special category for either favorable or adverse treatment. In *Kotch v. Bd. of River Port Com'rs for Port of New Orleans*,[147] a 1947 decision, the Supreme Court upheld by a 5–4 vote the practice of selecting riverboat pilots from among blood relatives of incumbent pilots. But the Court held that where such a legislature created a distinction among classes eligible for licensure, it would "consider the relationship of the method . . . to the broad objectives of the [law] . . . in the context of the historical evolution of the laws."[148]

The Court has applied this framework in more recent cases, exemplified by its 1985 decision in *City of Cleburne* v. *Cleburne Living Center*,[149] in which it struck down on equal protection grounds an ordinance requiring a special use permit for a home for mentally retarded persons. The Court applied a "rational basis" test, but because the ordinance departed from the Fourteenth Amendment's general "direction that all persons similarly situated should be treated alike,"[150] it conducted a two-pronged inquiry. First, the Court held, the government must show that the individuals in the group affected by the law possess "distinguishing characteristics"[151] that justify a "distinctive legislative response."[152] Second, the government must show the law actually is "based on [that] distinction."[153]

In *Cleburne*, the ordinance singled out homes for the mentally retarded as requiring a special use permit, while allowing a wide range of permissible uses such as apartments, nursing homes, boarding houses, and so forth. While conceding that the mentally retarded may possess some characteristics justifying some types of distinctive legislative treatment, the Court found that the government here failed to show that the "home and those who would occupy it would threaten legitimate interests of the city in a way that other permitted uses . . . would not." Without such a "special threat to the city's legitimate interests," the Court deemed the classification unconstitutional.[154]

Cleburne broke important new ground in the equal protection area. As one commentator has observed, "Because the Court has not clarified in what cases it will undertake to look behind asserted motives for impermissible ones, it appears open for plaintiffs to argue in every rational basis case that the particular statute in question was based on impermissible purposes."[155] Beyond finding some legislative classifications constitutionally impermissible, *Cleburne* requires "a 'tighter fit' between the means—the challenged classification—and the asserted ends" than in prior decisions.[156]

The *Cleburne* analysis is particularly applicable where a governmental entity permits some types of entrepreneurial opportunities but not other similar ones. *Cleburne* is also applicable if the governmental entity denies admission to a business or profession to some but not to others who are similarly situated. The litigator should argue this line of cases if the economic liberty interest at issue is subject to peculiar adverse legislative treatment.

Similarly, under the due process clause, the courts may strike down legislation that is too sweeping or oppressive. In *Moore* v. *City of East Cleveland*,[157] a case that could have been decided under the equal protection framework set forth in *Cleburne*, the Court struck down on substantive due process grounds a zoning law limiting occupancy of dwelling units to members of a nuclear family, thus prohibiting a grandmother from living with her grandson. (This case is an example of using favorable facts to challenge an oppressive law.) Writing for a plurality of four justices, Justice Powell stated that with regard to liberties protected by the due process clause, such as family choices, the Court "must examine carefully the importance of the governmental interests advanced and the extent to which they are served by the challenged regulation."[158] Powell acknowledged that the city's concerns about congestion, overcrowding, and the burden on city services were "legitimate," but he concluded that the ordinance was invalid since it served the city's objectives "marginally at best."[159]

Justice Powell did not define with specificity the liberty interests protected by due process, but quoted Justice John Harlan's definition of liberty as "a rational continuum which, broadly speaking, includes a freedom from all substantial arbitrary impositions and purposeless restraints."[160] Nor did Powell establish boundaries within which the scrutiny applied in *Moore* should extend. "Appropriate limits on substantive due process," Powell declared, "come not from drawing arbitrary lines but rather from careful 'respect for the teachings of history [and] solid recognition of the basic values that underlie our society.'"[161] Economic liberty should fit easily within the values outlined by Justice Powell and entitled to special protection under *Moore*.

Several recent lower court decisions have invalidated government regulations on equal protection and/or due process grounds. In *Sinaloa Lake Owners Ass'n* v. *City of Simi Valley*,[162] the Ninth Circuit applied a substantive due process analysis to a challenge by property owners to a city's decision to breach their dam. Analogizing the plaintiff's property deprivation to a criminal defendant's liberty interest in police brutality cases, Judge Alex Kozinski declared that "[t]o the extent that arbitrary or malicious use of physical force violates substantive due process, there is no principled basis for exempting the arbitrary or malicious use of other governmental powers from similar constitutional restraints."[163] Accordingly, Judge Kozinski set forth the applicable framework:

> [i]n determining whether the constitutional line has been crossed, a court must look to such factors as the need for the [governmental action], the relationship between the need and the [action taken], the extent of [damage] inflicted, and whether [the action was taken] in a good faith effort . . . or maliciously . . . for the very purpose of causing harm.[164]

This framework theoretically can be extended to protect against particularly egregious government conduct any of the liberty or property interests protected by the due process clause.

Similarly, in *Aladdin's Castle, Inc.* v. *City of Mesquite*, the Fifth Circuit invalidated on due process and equal protection grounds a municipal ordinance prohibiting minors from patronizing amusement establishments. The court found that the means employed—outright prohibition—were not tailored to the law's asserted objectives. The court declared that "[l]iberty stands for the idea that the government exists to serve the individual, not that the individual exists to be subservient to government or to a majority that controls government. The idea of liberty rejects governmental regimentation encompassing virtually every facet of the citizen's life."[165]

In *Brown* v. *Barry*, a federal district court struck down the District of Columbia's prohibition against sidewalk shoeshine stands. Applying *Cleburne*'s equal protection analysis, Judge

John H. Pratt concluded that "we would have to 'strain our imagination' beyond that which is required under the rational basis test to justify prohibiting bootblacks from the use of public space while permitting access to virtually every other type of vendor."[166]

In addition to due process and equal protection arguments, a litigator may also make arguments under the privileges or immunities clause without going so far as to ask a court to overrule *Slaughter-House*. Recall that in *Slaughter-House*, the Court held that the Fourteenth Amendment protected against state action only those privileges and immunities that are peculiar to national citizenship—that is, those rights that specifically "owe their existence to the Federal government, its national character, its Constitution, *or its laws*."[167] Whatever the status of economic liberty as an aspect of national citizenship at the time the Fourteenth Amendment was passed, the freedom to participate in the economy to the limits of individual merit and initiative is today firmly embedded in federal statutory law, particularly in the Sherman Act and Title VII. As Justice Thurgood Marshall has declared in the antitrust context,

> Antitrust laws . . . are the Magna Carta of free enterprise. They are as important to the preservation of economic freedom and our free enterprise system as the Bill of Rights is to the protection of our fundamental personal freedoms. And the freedom guaranteed each and every business, no matter how small, is the freedom to compete— to assert with vigor, imagination, devotion, and ingenuity whatever economic muscle it can muster.[168]

In essence, even if economic liberty was not a privilege and immunity of national citizenship at the time of *Slaughter-House*, it is arguable that the federal statutory expansion of economic liberty has rendered obsolete the *Slaughter-House* majority's modest inventory of privileges and immunities of national citizenship. Indeed, the Supreme Court has suggested as much, holding in a 1984 case that "the pursuit of a common calling is one of the most fundamental of those privileges protected by the [privileges and immunities] Clause" of Article IV, section 2.[169] Could it be that *Slaughter-House* has been effectively overruled by subsequent events? By defining the privileges and immunities of national citizenship subject to protection against the states by the Fourteenth Amendment as it did, the *Slaughter-House* majority left itself open to precisely such an attack.

These Fourteenth Amendment arguments provide a strong basis, along with other ancillary constitutional and statutory arguments suitable to specific fact patterns, for arguing economic liberty cases and developing favorable precedents, until such time as the issue is joined in such a way as to directly confront *Slaughter-House* and the defective jurisprudential doctrine it embodies.

FUTURE DIRECTIONS

In America's third century, the task of civil rights is to expand individual empowerment. If Americans like Alfredo Santos do not possess the right to earn an honest living in the calling of their choice, then Americans do not have civil rights.

The Supreme Court's abandonment of the privileges or immunities clause is one of the gravest abuses of judicial power in the history of American jurisprudence. The Court's failure to protect fundamental individual rights, including economic liberty, paved the way for *Plessy* v. *Ferguson* and for the denial of basic economic opportunities to the most disadvantaged in our society.

For a reinvigorated civil rights movement dedicated to individual empowerment, *Slaughter-House* is the rallying cry. The framers of the Fourteenth Amendment intended the privileges or immunities clause to protect the most fundamental rights of individuals and to act as an absolute restraint against government oppression. Like other constitutional guarantees that have been ignored by the courts, this guarantee has been consistently denied.

Since we are starting essentially at point zero, the years ahead provide enormous opportunities. It took the NAACP nearly a half century to dismantle separate but equal; it may take a long time to dismantle *Slaughter-House*. Surely it will take the same degree of tenacity, imagination, and passion. But once the battle is won, we will have secured for all Americans protection of their most sacred rights.

ENDNOTES

1. Antonin Scalia, "Economic Affairs as Human Affairs." In Dorn and Manne, p. 37.
2. *Slaughter-House Cases*, p. 111 (Field, J., dissenting).
3. *Santos* v. *City of Houston*, no. 89–1245 (S.D. Tex., filed 11 April 1989).
4. Murray, *Losing Ground.*
5. See, e.g., Bolick, *Changing Course*, pp. 104–12.
6. See, e.g., Robert H. Bork, *The Tempting of America* (New York: Free Press, 1990), p. 182.
7. Alfred Avins, ed., *The Reconstruction Amendments' Debates* (Wilmington, Del.: Delaware Law School, 1974), p. vii.
8. Dorn, p. 5.
9. Blackstone, p. 388.
10. Hayek, p. 19.
11. Belz, p. 109.
12. *Id.*
13. Dorn, p. 4.
14. See, e.g., Bork, pp. 36–49 and 223–29.
15. William Eaton, *Who Killed the Constitution?* (Washington: Regnery Gateway, 1988), p. 28.
16. *Id.*, p. 32.
17. *Id.*, p. 41.
18. Siegan, *The Supreme Court's Constitution*, p. 81.
19. For an extremely provocative debate on the proper role of the judiciary in protecting economic liberty, see *Scalia* v. *Epstein: Two Views on Judicial Activism* (Washington: Cato Institute, 1985).
20. Grimke, p. 392.
21. Spencer, p. 137.
22. Bolick, *Changing Course*, p. 25.
23. Report of Major General Carl Schurz on Condition of the South, 39th Cong., 1st Sess., 1865, Senate Exec. Doc. no. 2, p. 24; reproduced in Avins, p. 90.
24. *Cong. Globe*, 39th Cong., 1st Sess., 1866, H. pp. 1151–52.
25. Bolick, *Changing Course*, p. 26.
26. *Cong. Globe*, 39th Cong., 1st Sess., 1866, H. p. 1833.
27. *Id.*
28. *Id.*
29. Belz, p. 109.
30. *Id.*, p. 73.

31. *Cong. Globe*, 43rd Cong., 1st Sess., 1874, H. p. 413.
32. Belz, p. 121.
33. Curtis, p. 62.
34. *Id.*, p. 122.
35. *Cong. Globe*, 42nd Cong., 1st Sess., 1871, S. p. app. 228.
36. *Corfield* v. *Coryell*, 6 F. Cas. 546, 551–552 (C.C.E.D. Pa. 1823); cited in *Slaughter-House Cases*, p. 117 (Bradley, J., dissenting).
37. *Cong. Globe*, 43rd Cong., 1st Sess., 1874, S. p. 3454.
38. *Id.*
39. *Cong. Globe*, 39th Cong., 1st Sess., 1866, S. pp. 2765–66.
40. *Cong. Globe*, 42nd Cong., 1st Sess., 1871, S. p. 228.
41. Siegan, "Economic Liberties and the Constitution," pp. 141–42.
42. *Cong. Globe,* 42nd Cong., 2nd Sess., 1872, S. p. 843.
43. *Id.*, p. 844.
44. *Cong. Globe*, 42rd Cong., 1st Sess., 1871, H. p. app. 86.
45. *Cong. Globe*, 43rd Cong., 1st Sess., 1874, S. p. app. 363.
46. *Cong. Globe*, 42nd Cong., 2nd Sess., 1872, S. p. 762.
47. Joseph Tussman and Jacobus tenBroek, "The Equal Protection of the Laws," 37 *Cal. L. Rev.* 341, 342 (1949).
48. *Slaughter-House Cases*, pp. 59–60.
49. Charles A. Lofgren, *The Plessy Case* (New York: Oxford University Press, 1987), p. 67.
50. *Id.*, p. 85 (Field, J., dissenting).
51. *Id.*, p. 66 (majority).
52. *Id.*, p. 80.
53. Curtis, p. 173.
54. Quoted in Philip B. Kurland, "The Privileges or Immunities Clause: 'Its Hour Come Round at Last'?" 1972 *Wash. U. L.* Q. 405, 413 (1972).
55. *Slaughter-House Cases*, pp. 71–72 (majority).
56. *Dred Scott* v. *Sandford*, 60 U.S. 393 (1857).
57. *Slaughter-House Cases*, p. 73.
58. *Id.*, pp. 78–79.
59. *Id.*, pp. 79–80.
60. *Id.*, pp. 75–76.
61. *Id.*, p. 77.
62. *Id.*
63. *Id.*
64. *Id.*, p. 78.
65. Belz, p. 131.
66. Curtis, p. 176.

67. *Id.*, p. 175.
68. *Id.*, p. 173.
69. *Id.*, p. 177.
70. *Slaughter-House Cases,* p. 87 (Field, J., dissenting).
71. *Id.*, p. 88.
72. *Id.*, p. 89.
73. *Id.*, p. 93.
74. *Id.*, p. 96.
75. *Id.*
76. *Id.*, p. 101.
77. *Id.*
78. *Id.*, pp. 97–98.
79. *Id.*, p. 104.
80. *Id.*, p. 111.
81. *Id.*, p. 110.
82. *Id.*, p. 114 (Bradley, J., dissenting).
83. *Id.*, p. 112.
84. *Id.*, pp. 114–18.
85. *Id.*, p. 421.
86. *Id.*, pp. 119–20.
87. *Id.*, p. 426 (Swayne, J., dissenting).
88. *Id.*, p. 124.
89. *Id.*, p. 128.
90. *Id.*, p. 125.
91. *Id.*, pp. 128–29.
92. *Id.*, p. 129.
93. *Id.*, p. 130.
94. Avins, pp. xxx–xxxii.
95. *Cong. Globe*, 43rd Cong., 1st Sess., 1874, Senate, p. 4148.
96. Quoted in Curtis, p. 177.
97. *Changing Course*, p. 27.
98. *Bradwell* v. *The State*, 83 U.S. 130 (1872).
99. Avins, p. xxiv.
100. *Id.*, p. xxxii.
101. Bolick, *Changing Course*, pp. 32–33.
102. 118 U.S. 356 (1886).
103. *Id.*, p. 370.
104. 198 U.S. 45 (1905).
105. *Id.*, p. 53.
106. *Id.*, p. 57.
107. *Id.*, p. 56.

108. *Id.*, p. 64.

109. *Id.*, p. 59.

110. *Id.*, p. 75 (Holmes, J., dissenting).

111. Dorn, p. 9.

112. 300 U.S. 379 (1937).

113. *Adkins* v. *Children's Hospital*, 261 U.S. 525 (1923).

114. *West Coast Hotel*, p. 391.

115. *Id.*, p. 393.

116. *Id.*, p. 394.

117. *Id.*, p. 399.

118. *Id.*, pp. 399–400.

119. *Id.*, p. 402 (Sutherland, J., dissenting).

120. *Id.*, p. 413.

121. *Id.*, p. 406.

122. Norman Karlin, "Back to the Future: From *Nollan* to *Lochner*," 17 *Sw. U. L. Rev.* 627, 659 (1988).

123. 427 U.S. 297 (1976).

124. *Id.*, pp. 303–4.

125. Karlin, p. 660.

126. *Id.*

127. Leonard W. Levy, "Property as a Human Right," 5 *Const. Commentary* 169, 169 (1988).

128. *Id.*, p. 170.

129. *Id.*, p. 171.

130. *Id.* See also *Changing Course*, pp. 94–100; S. David Young, *The Rule of Experts* (Washington: Cato Institute, 1987); Walter Williams, *The State Against Blacks* (New York: McGraw–Hill Book Co., 1982).

131. Williams, p. 125.

132. Bolick, *Changing Course*, pp. 99–100.

133. Stuart Dorsey, "The Occupational Licensing Queue," 15 *J. of Human Resources* 425 (Summer 1980).

134. Bolick, *Changing Course*, p. 97.

135. Levy, p. 183.

136. Kurland, p. 406.

137. Karlin, p. 631.

138. Patrick O. Gudridge, "The Persistence of Classical Style," 131 *U. Pa. L. Rev.* 663, 710 (1983).

139. This point is argued in a forthcoming Note by David Bernstein entitled "The Supreme Court and Individual Rights, 1886–1908."

140. "Crisis in the Courts," p. 4.

141. See Richard A. Epstein, *Takings* (Cambridge: Harvard University Press, 1985).

142. See the as yet untitled book on property rights from the Center for Applied Jurisprudence of the Pacific Research Institute, forthcoming in 1990.

143. Kurland, p. 406.

144. *Id.,* pp. 418–20.

145. Barnett, p. 35.

146. For an excellent example, see Chlopecki, p. 74.

147. 330 U.S. 552 (1947).

148. *Id.,* p. 557.

149. 473 U.S. 432 (1985).

150. *Id.,* p. 439.

151. *Id.,* p. 441.

152. *Id.,* p. 443.

153. *Id.,* p. 449.

154. *Id.,* p. 448.

155. Note, "Still Newer Equal Protection: Impermissible Purpose Review in the 1984 Term," 53 *U. Chi. L. Rev.* 1454, 1482 (1986).

156. *Id.,* p. 1468.

157. 431 U.S. 494 (1977).

158. *Id.,* p. 499 (plurality).

159. *Id.,* p. 500.

160. *Id.,* p. 502 (quoting *Poe* v. *Ullman,* 367 U.S. 497, 543 (1961) (Harlan, J., dissenting).

161. *Id.,* p. 503 [citation omitted].

162. 864 F.2d 1475 (9th Cir. 1989).

163. *Id.,* p. 1485.

164. *Id.,* pp. 83–84 [brackets in original] (adapting from *Johnson* v. *Glick,* 414 U.S. 1028, 1033 (2d Cir.), *cert. denied,* 414 U.S. 1033 (1973)).

165. *Aladdin's Castle, Inc.* v. *City of Mesquite,* 630 F.2d 1029, 1045 (5th Cir. 1980), *rev'd in part and remanded,* 455 U.S. 283 (1982), *opinion extended,* 713 F.2d 137 (5th Cir. 1983).

166. *Brown* v. *Barry,* p. 356.

167. *Slaughter-House Cases,* p. 409 [emphasis added].

168. *United States* v. *Topco Assocs.,* 405 U.S. 596, 610 (1972).

169. *United Building & Construction Trades Council of Camden County and Vicinity* v. *Mayor and Council of the City of Camden,* 465 U.S. 208, 219 (1984).

Part III

TOPPLING *PLESSY V. FERGUSON:* INDIVIDUAL EMPOWERMENT THROUGH EQUALITY UNDER LAW

[Whenever we] depart from the principle of equal rights, or attempt any modification of it, we plunge into a labyrinth of difficulties from which there is no way out but by retreating. Where are we to stop? Or by what principle are we to find out the point to stop at, that shall discriminate between men of the same country, part of whom shall be free, and the rest not?

—Thomas Paine[1]

[W]e have accepted the sublime truths of the Declaration of Independence. We stand as the champions of human rights for all men, black and white, the wide world over, and we mean that just and equal laws shall pervade every rood of this nation; and when that is done our work ceases, but not until it is done.

—Senator Henry Wilson (1866)[2]

Demond Crawford, like many youngsters throughout America, was having trouble in school. His mother, Mary Amaya, was concerned; she decided to have her son tested.

Mrs. Amaya contacted the local public school district, which sent her a list of available tests, including the I.Q. test. But written across the bottom of the page were words that shocked Mrs. Amaya: your son may not take the I.Q. test because he is black.

93

Outraged, Mrs. Amaya contacted the NAACP for help in challenging this pernicious racial classification. But the NAACP officials not only refused to help Mrs. Amaya, they told her they were responsible for the adoption of the racial policy.

The school district offered a solution: since Demond is half black and half Hispanic, Mrs. Amaya could reclassify him from black to Hispanic, and he could take the test. Mrs. Amaya refused. She would not play games with her son's heritage to satisfy some social engineering bureaucrat.

The case of Demond Crawford conjures images of Homer Adolph Plessy, who was refused admission to the whites-only railroad car because he was one-eighth black. Once again, our government is allocating benefits and burdens on the basis of skin pigmentation and gradations thereof.

The California state policy that prevented Demond Crawford from taking an I.Q. test arose from a lawsuit in which the NAACP challenged the use of such tests as a screening device for pupil placements in special education classes. The plaintiffs argued the tests were biased against blacks.

The discrimination claim was never resolved by a trial, but the state agreed not to use the tests for special education placement. Later, however, the ban was extended to other uses of I.Q. tests, precluding black students from taking them but continuing to allow access to such tests to whites, Asians, Hispanics—everyone except blacks.

In her lawsuit against the state,[3] Mrs. Amaya takes no position on whether I.Q. tests are good or bad, or whether or not they discriminate against blacks; nor does she contend that the state has an obligation to provide I.Q. tests to anyone. She argues merely that if the state provides I.Q. tests, it must make them available without regard to race. A fairly modest argument, much like the ones civil rights groups used to make with some frequency.

The Crawford case illustrates why equality under law is so important to individual empowerment—and how far we have strayed from that objective. The principle of equality under law was embedded in our Constitution precisely to prevent special interest groups from invoking the coercive power of government to parcel out rights and privileges in an irrational or unequal manner.

And because race is inherently an irrational basis upon which to draw classifications, the notion of equality under law demands that the state treat individuals as individuals, not as a function of their race or skin color.

The Crawford case is only one of many throughout our nation's history in which the power of government was used to rearrange rights and privileges in a manifestly unequal manner. Sometimes these efforts were successful; other times, not. To the degree that the judiciary has acquiesced in these abuses, individual rights have suffered in kind, proving prophetic Tom Paine's warnings about departures from the absolute principle of equality under law.

Traditionally, the civil rights movement stood steadfastly for the principle of equality under law and sought consistently to vindicate it. A reinvigorated civil rights movement ought to commit itself to completing that task.

THE PRINCIPLES OF EQUALITY

The framers understood well the necessity of preventing the abuse of government power for the benefit of some and to the detriment of others. This theme was developed by James Madison in *The Federalist*, no. 10, in which he argued that one of the greatest benefits of republican government is "its tendency to break and control the violence of faction."[4] By "faction," Madison meant what is defined today as a special interest group:

> a number of citizens, whether amounting to a majority or minority of the whole, who are united and actuated by some common impulse of passion, or of interest, adverse to the rights of other citizens, or to the permanent and aggregate interests of the community.

To control the power of faction by limiting its liberty of operation, Madison maintained, is inconsistent with the principles of republican government. The better solution, Madison argued, is "controlling its effects" by rendering it "unable to concert and carry into effect schemes of oppression."

The framers sought to accomplish this goal through a number of constitutional provisions. As Jonathan Macey observes, "controlling the ability of interest groups to achieve anti-majoritarian outcomes in the legislature was a primary goal of the new Constitution,"[5] which "establishes a multitude of mechanisms to deter the efficacy of interest groups."[6] These provisions include the separation and balance of powers among the branches of government, the creation of an independent judiciary charged with the responsibility of protecting individual rights against deprivations by the legislative and executive branches,[7] the explicit enumeration of certain fundamental rights, and the specific limitation of government powers. Cass Sunstein notes that these specific limits on government power* are "united by a common theme and focused on a single underlying evil: the distribution of resources or opportunities to one group rather than another solely on the ground that those favored have exercised raw political power to obtain what they want."[8]

One of the most important of these mechanisms, the equal protection clause, was not formally incorporated into the Constitution until the Fourteenth Amendment. The framers probably thought it unnecessary; after all, the opening words of the Declaration of Independence established the equality of individuals in the context of their inalienable rights. As Thomas Paine argued, equality of rights was essential to the entire notion of rights.[9]

But, of course, this principle was profoundly violated for most of the following century through the institution of human slavery. Slavery demonstrated vividly the evil of faction and the necessity of equality under law: the subjugation of some individuals by others, effectuated by law that excluded protection of basic rights on the most irrational of justifications—race.

The framers of the Fourteenth Amendment sought to rectify this tragic departure from natural rights principles. They did so through the privileges or immunities and the due process clauses, extending protection of fundamental rights against the states. But they also specified that "No State shall ... deny to any person within its jurisdiction the equal protection of the laws."**

In the context of natural law principles that animated the amendment's enactment, the meaning of this provision was self-evident. The framers, nonetheless, made clear that the amendment

---

*These specific restraints on government power include the commerce, privileges and immunities, due process, equal protection, eminent domain, and contracts clauses.

**The Supreme Court has subsequently applied the equal protection guarantee to the federal government through the Fifth Amendment. See, e.g., *Bolling* v. *Sharpe*, 347 U.S. 497 (1954).

was designed to firmly establish the absolute principle of equality under law and to prevent government from using such characteristics as race as a basis for apportioning rights and privileges. Senator Jacob Howard declared that the intent of Congress was to "abolish all class legislation and do away with the injustice of subjecting one caste of persons to a code not applicable to another."[10] As Senator Thaddeus Stevens proclaimed, henceforth "no distinction would be tolerated in this purified Republic but what arose from merit or conduct."[11]

The amendment's architects distinguished between equality under law and equal outcomes. Representative Benjamin F. Butler, chairman of the House Judiciary Committee, drew the distinction sharply:

> I believe that "equal" in the Declaration of Independence is a political word, used in a political sense, and means equality of political rights. All men are not equal. Some are born with good constitutions, good health, strength, high mental power; others are not. Now, we cannot by legislation make them equal. God has not made them equal, with equal endowments.
>
> But this is our doctrine: Equality ... —and I will embody it in a single phrase, as the true touchstone of civil liberty—is not that all men are equal, *but that every man has the right to be the equal of every other man if he can.*[12]

Likewise, the amendment's framers intended the language of equality to embrace all individuals, regardless of color. As Senator Henry Wilson explained, "we have advocated the rights of the black man because the black man was the most oppressed"; but "we mean that the poorest man, be he black or white, ... is as much entitled to the protection of the law as the richest and the proudest man in the land[.]"[13] Accordingly, as Representative James F. Wilson declared, "In respect to all civil rights, ... there is to be hereafter no distinction between the white race and the black race."[14]

Thus conceived, the equal protection clause provides a powerful bulwark for individual self-determination. It does not prohibit the state from drawing reasonable distinctions in making public policy decisions. Rather, as Justice John Paul Stevens recently stated, the equal protection clause is a "direction that all persons similarly situated should be treated alike."[15] This line of demarcation prevents those who hold the reins of government power from preferring or excluding individuals for arbitrary, irrational, or unjust reasons. The clause does not referee the negotiation of entitlements among groups; it protects *individuals* against invidious attempts to rearrange rights or privileges to their detriment.

The equal protection clause does not create substantive rights or entitlements, nor does it ensure equal outcomes. Its command is simple. If government in its assignment of burdens or benefits *chooses* among individuals or groups, it must justify that choice. In some instances, that justification is easily supplied; in others, such as racial classifications, the burden is appropriately more difficult, if not impossible, to satisfy.

In its Fourteenth Amendment jurisprudence, the Supreme Court has constructed a general framework to determine whether the state has violated equal protection when it treats persons differently. If the challenged classification affects a fundamental right or is drawn upon a "suspect" classification (such as race), the Court subjects it to "strict" scrutiny, requiring that the government demonstrate that the classification is precisely tailored to a compelling state interest. If the challenged classification neither implicates fundamental rights nor is based on a suspect classification, the Court applies "rational basis" scrutiny. The Court has also applied an "intermediate" standard of scrutiny when the classification falls somewhere in the middle, such as gender-based distinctions.

The Supreme Court has departed from the principles of equal protection in three major respects. First, as Part 2 illustrates, the Court has failed to recognize as "fundamental" the full range of inalienable natural rights, such as private property rights and economic liberty, that the framers of the Fourteenth Amendment intended to protect. The Court should far more closely scrutinize classifications that affect such rights than it presently does.

Second, its "rational basis" scrutiny has, as a practical matter, typically amounted to complete deference to the state.[16] As a result, many governmental decisions that draw distinctions among groups or individuals in apportioning rights or privileges are insulated from judicial scrutiny, thereby frustrating the framers' objective of limiting the power of special interest groups.

Finally, the Court has failed to fully eradicate the use of racial classifications by government. The shameful persistence of racial classifications of one sort or another, along with the enormous costs to individual dignity sustained as a consequence of racial classifications, have combined to make race-related issues the preeminent feature of equal protection jurisprudence.

PLESSY AND THE ASSAULT ON EQUALITY UNDER LAW

The Fourteenth Amendment's promise of equality under law was dealt a tremendous setback in 1896 by the Supreme Court's decision in *Plessy* v. *Ferguson*, a case that demonstrates perhaps better than any other the necessity of restraints on the power of government to intervene in individual affairs.

In the quarter century following the Civil War, public transportation in the South was not rigidly segregated.[17] As historian Charles A. Lofgren recounts, over time, the white supremacists "realized that statutory law offered a tool for shaping relations between the races on public carriers." As a consequence, statutes mandating separate railroad cars for whites and blacks proliferated in the South during the late 1880s and early 1890s.[18]

In Louisiana, railroad companies opposed the state's "equal but separate" accommodations rule and rarely enforced it. Indeed, the Louisiana and Nashville Railroad agreed to assist in developing test cases to challenge the law.[19] One such test case involved Homer Adolph Plessy, who was one-eighth black. Plessy purchased a first-class rail ticket and refused his assignment to the colored car, whereupon he was imprisoned.

The Supreme Court sustained the law. Writing for the majority, Justice Henry B. Brown negated the plain meaning of the Fourteenth Amendment, declaring that

> [t]he object of the amendment was undoubtedly to enforce the absolute equality of the two races before the law, but, in the nature of things, it could not have been intended to abolish distinctions based upon color, or to enforce social, as distinguished from political, equality, or a commingling of the two races upon terms unsatisfactory to either. Laws permitting, and even requiring, their separation, in

places where they are liable to be brought into contact, do not necessarily imply the inferiority of either race to the other, and have been generally, if not universally, recognized as within the competency of the state legislatures in the exercise of their police power.[20]

In other words, equal protection of the laws did not require equal treatment under the law in all respects, but rather it permitted race-conscious legislation with respect to "social" concerns, which the Court defined to encompass such matters as education and inter-marriage.[21] In such areas, the Court ruled, race-based distinctions are valid if they are "reasonable," and "with respect to this there must necessarily be a large discretion on the part of the legislature."[22] Finding the statute reasonable, the Court upheld the statute.

Justice John M. Harlan was the sole dissenter, but his words would provide a rallying cry during the next 58 years for a civil rights movement determined to overturn the majority's tyrannical ruling. For Harlan, the statute was plainly "inconsistent with the personal liberty of citizens, white and black"; the decision to sustain it made a mockery of the "recent amendments of the supreme law, which established universal civil freedom, ... obliterated the race line from our systems of governments, national and state, and placed our free institutions upon the broad and sure foundation of the equality of all men before the law."[23] Harlan's dissent faithfully expressed the meaning and spirit of equal protection of the laws:

[I]n view of the constitution, in the eye of the law, there is in this country no superior, dominant, ruling class of citizens. There is no caste here. Our Constitution is color-blind, and neither knows nor tolerates classes among citizens. In respect of civil rights, all citizens are equal before the law. The humblest is the peer of the most powerful. The law regards man as man, and takes no account of his surroundings or of his color when his civil rights as guaranteed by the supreme law of the land are involved. It is therefore to be regretted that this high tribunal, the final expositor of the fundamental law of the land, has reached the conclusion that it is competent for a state to regulate the enjoyment by citizens of their civil rights solely upon the basis of race.[24]

For Justice Harlan, the principle of equality under law was absolute. And since no distinction in rights or privileges on the basis of race could be reasonable, no such classifications could be sustained.

Plessy neutralized the equal protection clause as a meaningful safeguard of individual rights against majoritarian abuses. It sanctioned the manipulation of the coercive power of government to achieve ends that could not be accomplished in a free market composed of autonomous individuals.

Nonetheless, the Court continued to approve such malevolent arrangements. In 1904, the Court upheld Kentucky's Day Law, which required racial segregation in private schools. Berea College, a private institution with an integrated student body, was fined $1,000 by the state, which the Court sustained as a proper exercise of the government's regulatory authority over corporations. Justice Harlan again dissented, charging that "the statute is an arbitrary invasion of the rights of liberty and property guaranteed by the Fourteenth Amendment against hostile state action, and is, therefore, void."[25] Harlan declared,

> Have we become so inoculated with prejudice of race that an American government, professedly based on the principles of freedom, and charged with the protection of all citizens alike, can make distinctions between such citizens in the matter of their voluntary meeting for innocent purposes simply because of their respective races?[26]

The most debilitating legacy of *Plessy*—one that continues to endure today—is the rejection of the absoluteness of equality under law. As Thomas Paine predicted, once the principle is compromised, it is no longer a viable principle. Charles Lofgren notes that the most troublesome aspect of these cases "was the 'reasonableness' test that judges applied to police regulations," which allowed courts to uphold the regulations on the basis of "supposed facts of race."[27]

Justice Robert Jackson sounded a similar concern nearly a half century after *Plessy* in his prophetic dissent to *Korematsu* v. *United States*,[28] in which the Supreme Court upheld the internment of United States citizens of Japanese ancestry. For Jackson, the principle of equality under law must be inviolable:

> [A] judicial construction ... that will sustain this order is a far more subtle blow to liberty than the promulgation of the order itself. ... [O]nce a judicial opinion rationalizes ... the Constitution to show that [it] sanctions such an order, the Court for all time has validated the principle of racial discrimination. ... The principle then lies about like a loaded weapon ready for the hand of any authority that can bring forward a plausible claim of an urgent need.[29]

That weapon has since been fired so many times, always with such tragic consequences, that we ought now endeavor to silence it once and for all.

Equality under law is an essential element of civil rights. A civil rights strategy based on individual empowerment must commit itself to restoring the vitality of the equal protection clause so that it may attain its intended status as a major bulwark of individual sovereignty.

TRIUMPH AND RETREAT

Perhaps never before in history has a movement worked so hard for so long to achieve a great triumph, only to abandon and repudiate its effort on the very threshold of victory, as did the NAACP in its allies and its half-century-long struggle to overturn *Plessy* v. *Ferguson* and everything it represented.

In 1954, Thurgood Marshall argued before the Supreme Court for the plaintiffs in *Brown* v. *Board of Education*, "That the Constitution is colorblind is our dedicated belief."[30] Only three decades later, Mary Frances Berry of the U.S. Commission on Civil Rights would attempt plausibly to argue that "[c]ivil rights laws were not passed to give civil rights protection to all Americans";[31] while NAACP executive director Benjamin Hooks would defend racial quotas by proclaiming that "[t]he Constitution was never color-blind."[32] Indeed, the most perverse irony of today's debate over racial classifications is that the defenders of quotas are in the position of advancing the principles embodied in the majority opinion in *Plessy*.

Indeed, *Brown* squarely presented two competing visions of equality under law. Thurgood Marshall's argument for the NAACP was a clarion call to natural law principles,* and he cast his lot unequivocally with the absolute principle of equality under law. Marshall declared that "so far as our argument on the constitutional debate is concerned ... the state is deprived of any power to make any racial classification in any governmental field." In Marshall's view, "It is the dissenting opinion of Justice Harlan, rather than the majority opinion in *Plessy* v. *Ferguson*, that is in keeping with the scope and meaning of the Fourteenth Amendment."[33]

Marshall won the battle in *Brown*—the doctrine of "separate but equal" was repudiated—but he failed to win the argument. That distinction is the source of our subsequent inability to resolve once and for all the question of government's power to enact racial classifications.

Conventional wisdom holds that *Brown* overturned *Plessy*; in a technical sense, that is true. What *Brown* did not do is explicitly to repudiate the rationale underlying *Plessy*, namely that racial classifications are permissible if they are "reasonable." Also *Brown* did not embrace the dissenting opinion of Justice Harlan. The closest the Court came to vindicating the core principle of the equal protection clause was to declare that education, "where the state has undertaken to provide it, is a right which must be made available to all on equal terms."[34] But rather than striking down the law as committing on its face an obvious violation of that principle, it conducted what amounted to a "reasonableness" inquiry into the importance of education[35] and the effects of school segregation on blacks[36] to support its conclusion that "[s]eparate educational facilities are inherently unequal."[37] As Charles Lofgren views it, *Brown* "did not reject reliance on racial 'facts,' a central ... feature of Justice Brown's reasoning in *Plessy*. Nor did the judges wholeheartedly embrace Justice Harlan's color-blind Constitution. The *Brown* case itself hinted that the spirit of *Plessy* survived in these regards."[38]

*Indeed, the NAACP's brief in *Brown* is probably the most comprehensive summary of the natural law origins of civil rights ever written.

William B. Allen remarks that "*Brown* spoke of, without accomplishing, the overturning of *Plessy* v. *Ferguson*, with the result that, 'today the *Brown* decision is considered the progenitor of a host of color-conscious and group-specific policies.'"[39] The failure of the Court to adopt Justice Harlan's dissenting opinion in *Plessy*, Allen argues, means that "in spite of *Brown*, we struggle still with the question about the just means to implement standards of equality and fairness in American life."[40] By leaving at least partly intact the "reasonableness" inquiry set forth by the *Plessy* majority, the Court thus retained a framework for rationalizing invidious discrimination that continues to rear its ugly head to this day.

The remedy chosen to implement *Brown* exacerbated these problems. Instead of striking down enforced legal separation and acting to ensure meaningful individual choice, such as through an award of monetary damages, the Court approved forced busing with the goal of attaining racial balance. Instead of vindicating the equal right of every individual to pursue educational opportunities, the Court made paramount the perceived right of groups to attain racial balance. Within 10 years after *Brown*, the transition from the goal of equality of opportunity to forced equality in result was complete.

A similar metamorphosis occurred in the context of the landmark civil rights legislation of the 1960s. Like Marshall's argument in *Brown*, the framers of the Civil Rights Act consistently invoked the traditional principles of civil rights, making clear their intent to remove the ugly blot of discrimination from the free-enterprise system while leaving its dynamic mechanisms otherwise intact. Senator Gordon Allott, for instance, described the law's goal as a society in which decisions were based on merit and "the color of a man's skin ... [is] completely extraneous."[41] Describing the law's practical ramifications, Senator Hubert Humphrey, the primary sponsor, declared that Title VII "does not limit the employer's freedom to hire, fire, promote, or demote for any reasons—or for no reasons—so long as his action is not based on race."[42]

The act's supporters also emphasized that the law prohibited discrimination against *anyone* on the basis of race. One of the act's co-sponsors, Senator Thomas Kuchel, proclaimed "the bill ... is color-blind."[43] Thus, they viewed the bill as incompatible with racial quotas since, as Senator Thomas Clark noted, "Quotas are themselves discriminatory."[44] Senator Harrison Williams, another co-sponsor, may have phrased the question most pointedly: "[H]ow can the language of equality favor one race ... over another?" asked Williams, adding that "[t]hose who say that equality means favoritism do violence to commonsense."[45]

As described in Part 1, the years since the passage of the 1964 act, however, have witnessed the wholesale abandonment of the core principles and unifying objectives that delivered the civil rights movement to this threshold of victory. Nathan Glazer summarizes this remarkable transformation:

> In 1964, we declared that no account should be taken of race, color, national origin, or religion in the spheres of voting, jobs, and education. ... Yet no sooner had we made this national assertion than we entered into an unexampled recording of the color, race, and national origin ... in every significant sphere of [a person's] life. Having placed into law the dissenting opinion of *Plessy* v. *Ferguson* that our Constitution is color-blind, we entered into a period of color-and group-consciousness with a vengeance.[46]

By replacing the goal of equality of opportunity with forced equality of result, we have transformed a strategy that expands opportunities into a zero-sum game: one person's gain is necessarily another person's loss. Such a shift, Morris Abram argues, reduces the noble quest for civil rights into "a crude political struggle between groups seeking favored status."[47] This result is precisely the opposite of what the framers sought to accomplish in ensuring equality under law.

Sadly, we may today be farther away than we were in 1954 from the day in which the constitutional promise of equality under law is finally fulfilled. Never was the moral imperative clearer than it was in the days of *Brown*; never was the national consensus as broad as it was at the passage of the Civil Rights Act 10 years after *Brown*.

If Thurgood Marshall's argument had prevailed in *Brown*, surely America's racial landscape would look much different today. Perhaps it would resemble, much more than it does, the vision expressed by Martin Luther King of a land inhabited by autonomous individuals living in racial harmony. We have lost so much ground, so much momentum, so much of the consensus that sustained the mission for equal opportunity, that we may never reclaim it. Yet the ever-deepening miasma in which we are mired as a consequence of compromising the principle of equality of law— a morass predicted with remarkable clarity by Thomas Paine, Abraham Lincoln, Robert Jackson, and others—reiterates the importance of continuing the fight to once and for all consign *Plessy* and all it stands for to the dustbin of history.

ERADICATING RACIAL CLASSIFICATIONS AND PRESUMPTIONS

W.E.B. DuBois proclaimed in 1903 that "[t]he problem of the twentieth century is the problem of the color-line."[48] This question—the extent to which the rights of individuals depend on their race or color—continues to face us as America reaches the twilight of the 20th century. Individuals cannot secure control over their destinies while the government possesses the power to apportion rights and privileges on the basis of unjust, arbitrary, or irrational justifications—including and especially race.

These issues are perhaps most pronounced in three race-related contexts: racial classifications, the "adverse impact" doctrine, and educational opportunities. In recent years, a recognition of the problems resulting from the abandonment of traditional civil rights principles has increasingly influenced public policy and judicial decisions. In particular, the Supreme Court recently has taken tentative, but important, steps to restore vigor to the concept of equality under law. What follows is a summary of the law's development in each of these three areas, as well as an outline of litigation strategies designed to build upon recent positive trends and to advance the principle of equality under law.

Racial Classifications: The Progeny of Plessy

Nowhere has the retreat from principles been more pronounced than in the civil rights establishment's toleration of—indeed, its insistence on—racial classifications. As a result, the philosophical battle lines are sharply drawn over what Eleanor Holmes Norton, former chairperson of the U.S. Equal Employment Opportunity

Commission and one of the foremost architects of the contemporary forms of racial classifications, euphemistically calls
"conceptual innovations in equality mechanisms."[49]

As discussed in Part 1, and specifically in the case of young Mark
Anthony Nevels, it is not at all clear that quotas always help their
supposed beneficiaries. The notion that each person enters life with
a racial passport is tremendously damaging to every member of
society.[50] Once the protection of equality under law is compromised
for one person, it is subject to compromise for any person.

No less a liberal than Justice William O. Douglas warned in
DeFunis v. *Odegaard* that the Fourteenth Amendment's guarantees would lose their meaning "[i]f discrimination based on race is
constitutionally permissible when those who hold the reins can
come up with 'compelling' reasons to justify it."[51] But in *Regents of
the University of California* v. *Bakke*,[52] the first "reverse
discrimination" case in which it rendered a decision on the merits,
the Supreme Court declined to heed this warning; instead it
exposed, in almost exaggerated fashion, the consequences of its
failure to embrace absolute principles. The Court was badly
fragmented, with five justices voting to strike down the racial
quota for admissions to the medical school of the University of
California–Davis, but without a single justice joining fully Justice
Lewis F. Powell's swing-vote opinion.

Justice Powell's opinion, however, set the tone for the Court's
decisions for at least the next 11 years. Justice Powell seemed to
embrace the spirit of the Fourteenth Amendment when he declared
that the "guarantee of equal protection cannot mean one thing
when applied to one individual and something else when applied to
a person of another color. If both are not accorded the same
protection, then it is not equal."[53] Accordingly, he set forth the
"strict scrutiny" standard, proclaiming that "[r]acial and ethnic
distinctions of any sort are inherently suspect and thus call for the
most exacting judicial examination."[54] Stripping the admissions
policy of its benevolent facade, Justice Powell stated the issue with
clarity: the quota's defenders, he charged,

> urge us to adopt for the first time a more restrictive view of the Equal
> Protection Clause and hold that discrimination against members of the
> white "majority" cannot be suspect if its purpose can be characterized

as "benign." The clock of our liberties, however, cannot be turned back to 1868. . . . It is far too late to argue that the guarantee of equal protection to *all* persons permits the recognition of special wards entitled to a degree of protection greater than that accorded others.[55]

Yet Powell went on to construct hypothetical instances in which a state permissibly could confer benefits and burdens on the basis of race,[56] thus exacerbating the very confusion that allowed the quota issue to arise in the first place.

For their part, the dissenters made clear their view that discrimination against certain "classes" required only an inquiry into "whether race is reasonably used"—the very same construct applied in *Plessy*.[57] Reminding his brethren that "no decision of this Court has ever adopted the proposition that the Constitution must be colorblind,"[58] Brennan rejected any "static definition of discrimination."[59] Thus loosening the equal protection clause from any principled moorings, Brennan could conclude that quotas were permissible "where there is a sound basis for concluding that minority underrepresentation is substantial and chronic."[60] After all, Brennan reasoned, "no fundamental right is involved here" since "whites as a class" were not victimized by past discrimination.[61]

Brennan's dissent gave voice to a number of themes that would supply the theoretical framework for this species of racial classifications. First, of course, Brennan viewed the equal protection clause as something much less than absolute and giving significant protection only to some people and in some circumstances. Brennan contended the clause protects disadvantaged "classes," not individuals. For such disadvantaged classes, reparations (such as quotas) are justified; the Fourteenth Amendment does not require a showing of continuing discrimination to sustain such measures, but merely a showing of "underrepresentation" (i.e., statistical disparities).

While Justice Brennan was crafting a coherent, if defective, rationale for a vastly reconstructed equal protection clause, Justice Harry Blackmun was displaying the frightening illogic inherent in such an exercise, asserting that "[i]n order to get beyond racism, we must first take account of race. . . . And in order to treat some persons equally, we must treat them differently."[62] In this remarkable statement by Blackmun, district court Judge Stewart

Newblatt would later observe, "Orwell would have found grist for his mill."[63]

But the abandonment of the principle of nondiscrimination was perhaps best exemplified by Justice Thurgood Marshall's dissent, in which Marshall repudiated the views he had once championed and trivialized the importance of Justice Harlan's bold dissent in *Plessy*, remarking that "[w]e must remember . . . that the principle that the 'Constitution is color-blind' appeared only in the opinion of the lone dissenter."[64]

For the next decade, the Court was largely paralyzed by its equivocation. Justice Powell (later joined by Justice Sandra Day O'Connor) continued to provide the swing vote; Justices John Paul Stevens (an early quota critic who is now generally a supporter) and Byron White (who signed on to Justice Brennan's *Bakke* dissent but is now a staunch opponent of quotas) essentially switched sides. The Court's decisions during this period produced mixed results under both the Fourteenth Amendment and Title VII,[65] with several upholding racial classifications, such as *Fullilove* v. *Klutznick* (federal contract set-asides),[66] *United Steelworkers* v. *Weber* (private sector quota),[67] *Local 28, Sheet Metal Workers* v. *EEOC* (court-imposed quota),[68] *United States* v. *Paradise* (same),[69] and *Johnson* v. *Transportation Agency* (voluntary public sector quota analyzed solely under Title VII).[70] A few decisions struck them down, including *Firefighters Local Union No. 1784* v. *Stotts* (court-ordered quota),[71] and *Wygant* v. *Jackson Board of Education* (public sector quota).[72] Nonetheless, lower federal courts during this period routinely upheld racial classifications, some of them explicitly adopting as law the reasonableness standard embodied in Justice Brennan's *Bakke* dissent.[73]

A firm consensus seems to have emerged, however, during the most recent Supreme Court term. In *City of Richmond* v. *J. A. Croson Co.*,[74] an outright majority of the Court for the first time applied a strict scrutiny standard for assessing racial classifications and firmly repudiated Justice Brennan's reasonableness construct. By a 6–3 vote (with five justices joining the relevant portions of Justice O'Connor's opinion), the Court struck down a 30 percent minority set-aside for public contracts since the city "failed to demonstrate a compelling interest in apportioning public contracting opportunities on the basis of race,"[75] and because the quota was not "narrowly tailored to remedy prior discrimination."[76]

With respect to the first part of this two-part analysis, Justice O'Connor declared that "an amorphous claim that there has been past discrimination in a particular industry cannot justify the use of an unyielding racial quota."[77] Such a rationale, O'Connor explained, would

> open the door to competing claims for "remedial relief" for every disadvantaged group. The dream of a Nation of equal citizens in a society where race is irrelevant to personal opportunity and achievement would be lost in a mosaic of shifting preferences based on inherently unmeasurable claims of past wrongs. . . . We think such a result would be contrary to both the letter and spirit of a constitutional provision whose central command is equality.[78]

Likewise, O'Connor concluded the quota was not "narrowly tailored" since it apparently was designed not to remedy past discrimination but to ensure "outright racial balancing," and because the city failed to consider nonracial mechanisms to achieve its goals.[79]

In an opinion concurring in the judgment, Justice Antonin Scalia criticized his colleagues for leaving intact the view "that, despite the Fourteenth Amendment, state and local governments may in some circumstances discriminate on the basis of race."[80] The Constitution guarantees racial neutrality, Scalia argued, warning that "[w]hen we depart from this American principle we play with fire, and much more than an occasional DeFunis, Johnson, or Croson burns."[81] Scalia explained that "[i]n my view there is only one circumstance in which the States may act *by race* to 'undo the effects of past discrimination': where that is necessary to eliminate their own maintenance of a system of unlawful racial classification"[82] This limitation is essential, Scalia argued:

> The difficulty of overcoming the effects of past discrimination is as nothing compared with the difficulty of eradicating from our society the source of those effects, which is the tendency—fatal to a nation such as ours—to classify and judge men and women on the basis of their

country of origin or the color of their skin. A solution to the first problem that aggravates the second is no solution at all.[83]

The Constitution thus requires nonracial means to cure disadvantages attributable in whole or part to past discrimination. As Scalia reasoned,

> those who believe that racial preferences can help to "even the score" display, and reinforce, a manner of thinking by race that was the source of the injustice and that will, if it endures within our society, be the source of more injustice still. The relevant proposition is not that it was blacks, or Jews, or Irish who were discriminated against, but that it was individual men and women, "created equal," who were discriminated against. And the relevant resolve is that that should never happen again.[84]

"Since blacks have been disproportionately disadvantaged by racial discrimination," Scalia continued, "any race-neutral remedial program aimed at the disadvantaged *as such* will have a disproportionately beneficial impact on blacks. Only such a program, and not one that operates on the basis of race, is in accord with the letter and the spirit of our Constitution."[85]

Justice Anthony Kennedy, concurring separately, agreed with Justice Scalia that the "moral imperative of racial neutrality is the driving force of the Equal Protection Clause."[86] But "[o]n the assumption that it will vindicate the principle of race neutrality," Kennedy stated that he would "accept the less absolute rule contained in Justice O'Connor's opinion, a rule based on the proposition that any racial preference must face the most rigorous scrutiny by the courts." While thus declining to adopt Justice Scalia's bright-line equal protection framework "at this point,"[87] Justice Kennedy served notice that he looks favorably upon Scalia's construct and will embrace it if strict scrutiny proves an inadequate safeguard for the principle of equality under law.

The Court's decision in *Croson* places the quest for equality in a much better position than the Court found it: a majority of the Court is in agreement that strict scrutiny applies to all racial classifications, and apparently that racial classifications can survive such scrutiny only under the most exceptional circumstances. And its decisions are apparently sending a clear message: since *Wygant*, whose plurality opinion set forth the standards later adopted by the *Croson* majority, lower courts have fairly uniformly struck down racial classifications.[88]

The battle is not fully won, however. Until the Supreme Court adopts Justice Harlan's dissenting opinion in *Plessy*—most recently articulated by Justice Scalia's concurring opinion in *Croson*—the principle of equality under law is subject to compromise. Moreover, many well-intentioned people still confuse racial quotas with concepts such as equal opportunity and affirmative action.* Until the confusion is clarified over precisely what equality under law means—and why it is vital for the protection of individual liberty—we are in grave danger of witnessing the further erosion of that principle's central importance in our constitutional scheme.

Effective litigation taking *Croson* as the baseline is therefore crucial. The Court's decision the same term in *Martin* v. *Wilks*[89] made clear that parties to litigation cannot bargain away the rights of third parties who are not before the court, meaning that the courthouse doors will not be closed by procedural technicalities to civil rights plaintiffs who are challenging racial classifications.

Such litigation may take several forms, including continued challenges to racial quotas and minority set-asides. Simultaneously, advocates of equality under law should recognize that many in our society have never enjoyed full equality of opportunity, and they should accompany their attacks on racial classifications with constructive proposals to eradicate barriers to opportunity.

Perhaps the most fruitful strategy for fulfilling the promise of equality under law is targeting litigation to highlight the perverse by-products of "benevolent" racial classifications. Since quotas and set-asides are necessarily a zero-sum game, the "losers" are composed of all those who are not within the preferred groups, and their

---

*Opposition to racial quotas by no means is the same as opposition to "affirmative action," in the original and highest meaning of that term. As Justice Scalia emphasized in his *Croson* opinion, government is free to act in race-neutral ways to help the disadvantaged. Quotas, as noted earlier, tend to channel benefits to the most advantaged members of the designated groups, thus leaving intact the serious problems suffered by the most disadvantaged individuals, such as inadequate educational skills, welfare dependency, crime, and barriers to entrepreneurial opportunities. True affirmative action means eliminating arbitrary barriers to opportunity and giving people the tools to overcome these disadvantages. See, for example, Bolick and Nestleroth.

numbers may well include individuals who are now doubly handicapped by a quota. Likewise, rigid quotas often impose limits of one sort or another on the intended beneficiaries.

As race-consciousness grows more pervasive, the number of examples of perverse consequences grows. For instance, some universities apparently have established "ceilings" on admissions for Asian-American applicants, despite their demonstrable qualifications, since their group is "overrepresented."[90] Similarly, in a number of cases, the use of quotas not to secure additional opportunities but to achieve a particular racial balance often produces ceilings on opportunities. In the area of public housing, for instance, the widespread practice of "integration maintenance" operates in the name of racial balance to leave housing units vacant in search of white tenants instead of providing the units to black applicants who are turned away solely because of their color.[91]

In championing the principle of equality under law, plaintiffs in these types of cases are often tactically preferable to the proverbial "white firefighters" in a number of respects. First, the plaintiffs cannot be accused in any manner of having been the beneficiaries of past discrimination in their favor. Indeed, they typically are disadvantaged people themselves, who now have their opportunities circumscribed by a racial quota. Second, their plight underscores the inherent futility of any attempted "middle ground" in the realm of racial classifications, proving correct the prophetic warnings of such justices as John Harlan, Robert Jackson, William O. Douglas, and Antonin Scalia. Finally, they divide and confuse the civil rights leadership elite, which knows it likes quotas and racial balance but is surely flustered when those devices harm their own constituency. Specific examples of such cases are profiled in the appendix.

Creative litigation in this area will eventually destroy the tenuous philosophical underpinnings of *Plessy* by demonstrating vividly that racial classifications are *never* reasonable. The wisdom of the framers of the Fourteenth Amendment in crafting an absolute guarantee of equality under law has and will continue to stand the test of time. Our task is to vindicate that wisdom.

The Engine of Quotas: Adverse Impact and Statistical Mischief

The most potent weapon in the battle to transform equal opportunity into forced equality of results is the "adverse impact" doctrine, the legal theory by which plaintiffs may prove discrimination on the basis of statistical disparities among racial or ethnic groups. Since its first appearance in 1971 in *Griggs* v. *Duke Power Co.*,[92] the adverse impact doctrine has developed, as Earl M. Maltz describes it, into "perhaps the single most dominant feature of antidiscrimination law in America";[93] the perversion of that doctrine has turned adverse impact into a powerful engine of quotas.

Quota defenders often claim that many employers, public and private, adopt quotas "voluntarily." Eleanor Holmes Norton, who headed the EEOC as it embraced and implemented racial quotas, is one who claims that "[g]oals and timetables became pervasive in employment through voluntary employer action." But this "voluntary" development, Norton recounts, was "encouraged by federal court precedents" and "generated by the government in its enforcement of Executive Order 11246, which requires goals and timetables of government contractors."[94] Indeed, the saga of contemporary racial quotas is one of subtle yet effective government coercion, using an antidiscrimination statute to compel discrimination.

That the framers of the Civil Rights Act intended no such result is apparent not only from their repeated assurances of broad employer discretion over employment practices, but also by the express language of Title VII. Section 703(j) provides that the law does not require

> preferential treatment to any individual or group . . . on account of an imbalance which may exist with respect to the total or percentage of persons of any race, color, religion, sex, or national origin employed . . . in any comparison with the total number or percentage in any community . . . or in the available workforce. . . .

Section 703(h) further provides that it shall not "be an unlawful practice for an employer to give and to act upon the results of any professionally developed ability test provided such test . . . is not designed, intended, or used to discriminate. . . ."

The legislative history and language thus make it clear that Title VII was not intended to require employers to abandon nondiscriminatory employment practices or to seek racially balanced workforces. But as Norton observes, the Supreme Court, "finding little to guide it, took charge of the statute."[95]

As originally announced in *Griggs*, the adverse impact doctrine did not conflict with the intent of Title VII. Prior to *Griggs*, the only method by which to prove discrimination in the absence of direct evidence of discriminatory intent was "disparate treatment"—that is, situations in which similarly situated persons of different races are treated differently, which gives rise to a rebuttable presumption that the explanation for the different treatment is discrimination.

But not all situations are amenable to disparate treatment analysis. *Griggs* presented the question of whether an employer's requirement of either a high school diploma or a passing score on a standardized general intelligence test was permissible when "(a) neither standard is shown to be significantly related to successful job performance, (b) both requirements operate to disqualify Negroes at a substantially higher rate than white applicants, and (c) the jobs in question formerly had been filled by white employees as part of a longstanding practice of giving preference to whites."[96]

The Court's answer, not surprisingly, was no; the job requirements, which produced adverse racial impact but did not predict "a reasonable measure of job performance,"[97] the Court concluded, "operate[d] to 'freeze' the status quo of prior discriminatory employment practices."[98] Since "[w]hat is required by Congress is the removal of artificial, arbitrary, and unnecessary barriers to employment when the barriers operate invidiously to discriminate,"[99] the Court ruled the employment requirements invalid under Title VII.

The adverse impact theory as outlined in *Griggs* provides a logical means of ferreting out "covert" instances of discrimination. For example, an all-white community that is surrounded by black suburbs and that adopts a residency requirement for municipal jobs is fairly obviously engaging in racial discrimination if it cannot show a business purpose for its requirement.[100]

But this rational application of adverse impact to uncover hidden discriminatory practices was quickly expanded into a device by which employers were held liable for discrimination whenever they used employment criteria that produced statistical disparities. This evolution progressed from the presumption, articulated by the Court in its 1977 *Teamsters* decision, that "absent explanation, it is ordinarily to be expected that nondiscriminatory hiring practices will in time result in a work force more or less representative of the racial or ethnic composition of the population in the community from which employees are hired."[101] This presumption was hopelessly flawed;[102] given the range of possible explanations for statistical disparities—individual preferences and variations in age, qualifications, interest, information, location, education, and so on—mere statistics without more do not logically support a significant inference of discrimination except in a broader *Griggs*-type context supplying additional evidence of discrimination. Nonetheless, this presumption fueled efforts to turn Title VII into a guarantee of equal outcomes for groups.

Indeed, the courts and the Equal Employment Opportunity Commission (EEOC) acted as if *Griggs* were a line of scrimmage from which to march the football steadily downfield. The cases established a three-part adverse impact analysis: (1) plaintiffs could establish a *prima facie* case of discrimination solely on the basis of statistical disparities, (2) the employer would then have to prove the business necessity of its practices, and (3) the plaintiff could rebut such a defense by showing it was pretextual.[103] The EEOC's guidelines went even further, requiring the employer to show that no alternative selection device is available that would produce less adverse impact.[104]

In addition to allowing plaintiffs to prove their cases on purely statistical showings without requiring any evidence whatsoever of the employer's intent to discriminate, the courts and EEOC made it nearly impossible for employers to prove their practices were justified by "business necessity." Departing from the *Griggs* standard of a "reasonable measure of job performance," lower courts required employers to demonstrate that the challenged job practice was "essential"[105] or justified by an "irresistible demand."[106]

In the context of employment tests, this standard required "validation" by test experts to show a precise correlation between the test and job performance, a process that often runs into hundreds of thousands of dollars.[107] As one district court judge complained in 1973, "Under this rigid standard, there is no test known or available today which meets the Equal Employment Opportunity Commission requirements for any industry."[108] Justice Harry Blackmun later warned, "I fear that a too-rigid application of the EEOC Guidelines will leave the employer little choice, save an impossibly expensive and complex validation study, but to engage in a subjective quota system of employee selection. This, of course, is far from the intent of Title VII."[109]

Indeed, such a result conflicts both with section 703(j) of Title VII, which precludes requiring employers to adopt racial preferences to eliminate statistical disparities, and 703(h), which protects nondiscriminatory testing devices. Yet the fears expressed by Justice Blackmun were fully realized. As Michael Gold charges, "Quotas and adverse impact are practically synonymous. In theory, an employer can win an adverse impact case by proving that the challenged selection criterion is valid. In practice, this burden can almost never be carried, and the result is that employers are forced to hire and promote by quotas."[110]

Employers have also routinely abandoned tests rather than defending them. A survey by the Equal Employment Advisory Council found that 82 percent of its corporate members had ceased the use of some or all tests because they fear litigation or the cost of validation.[111] This abandonment of standards leads to substantial losses in industrial productivity and competitiveness.[112]

Defenders of the most extreme applications of adverse impact contend that discrimination is difficult to detect without reliance on statistics and that, if adverse impact doctrine is modified, many instances of discrimination will escape detection and elude remedy.

The response to this claim relies in part on the definition of discrimination. If discrimination means nothing more than statistical racial disparity, adverse impact analysis is appropriate in all cases. But if discrimination means treating people differently on the basis of race or other irrelevant characteristics, then adverse impact and statistics are of limited usefulness. Certainly, statistics are relevant in drawing or buttressing inferences of discrimination in many cases. But when plaintiffs rely solely on statistics, that means they have produced no evidence that the employer is treating similarly situated persons differently, which is the essence of discrimination as that term is normally understood. In other words, adverse impact cases do not involve people who are being treated *differently*; rather, they are cases in which people are treated *the same*, but with statistically different outcomes.

One logically would expect that the law would deal less harshly with an employer who treats everyone the same than it would deal with an employer who treats people differently. But in practice precisely the opposite is true. Adverse impact thus encourages employers to abandon objective standards in favor of subjective mechanisms, even though subjective mechanisms are much more susceptible to discriminatory influences.

This phenomenon is bizarre in light of Title VII's objectives, but it is not coincidental. The revisionists' civil rights agenda requires the abandonment of objective standards in order to produce proportional results. This misuse of adverse impact is a classic example of using the coercive power of government to redistribute rights and privileges, at substantial cost to equal opportunity.

Yet no assurance exists that this redistributionist agenda does much to secure real progress for its intended beneficiaries. By characterizing every racial disparity as discrimination that is curable by a quota, the revisionists' construct glosses over and leaves unsolved enormous problems among the economically disadvantaged. Most importantly, by replacing the requirement of individual achievement with a regime of entitlements and by applying different standards to different groups, this construct does nothing to provide the most disadvantaged with the tools necessary to satisfy objective standards of performance or to effectively compete in the real world. Indeed, as Judge Clarence Thomas has charged, the revisionists' approach tacitly validates notions of the "inherent inferiority of blacks ... by suggesting that they should not be held to the same standards as other people."[113]

Moreover, by its reliance on outcomes, this construct allows an easy out to those who are guilty of discrimination, for quotas do not require an employer to do anything differently except to hire or promote different people. Quotas do nothing to break the habit of discriminating on the basis of race, nor do they encourage meaningful efforts to invest in those who are outside the economic mainstream. The experience of 25 years of quotas reveals them to be a superficial remedy that does little to help the most disadvantaged.[114]

That we have suffered from such experiences is attributable to the willingness of the courts to adopt the revisionists' adverse impact construct. As Earl M. Maltz observes, adverse impact "seems to have been adopted almost as a reflex, with no thought apparently given to the implications ... and problems.[115] Even more ominously, adverse impact has been extended beyond the employment context to such areas as voting rights,[116] housing discrimination,[117] and age discrimination,[118] with predictably harmful results.

Fortunately, the Supreme Court has recently embarked upon a more moderate and reasonable course of action, signaling that the adverse action mischief may have run its course. In its 1989 decision in *Wards Cove Packing Co.* v. *Atonio*,[119] the Court made significant strides in harmonizing adverse impact doctrine with the intent of Title VII.

The plaintiffs in *Atonio* challenged an employer's entire range of hiring practices, relying solely on statistics that showed a high percentage of nonwhite workers in certain unskilled jobs and a high percentage of whites in skilled jobs. (The plaintiffs also challenged certain practices on "disparate treatment" grounds, but these were not before the Court.) The Ninth Circuit Court of Appeals had ruled below that the plaintiffs' statistical showing was adequate to establish a *prima facie* showing of discrimination and that the burden shifted to the employer to prove the business necessity of its practices.[120]

The Supreme Court reversed in a 5–4 decision written by Justice Byron White. The Court first focused on the use of statistics in establishing a *prima facie* case; it then concluded that the comparison of one category of jobs with different jobs was not probative of discrimination. Rather, the Court ruled, the plaintiffs must produce statistics with respect to "'the pool of *qualified* job applicants' or the *'qualified* population in the labor force'" to establish a showing of possible discrimination.[121] Otherwise, Justice White explained,

> any employer who had a segment of his work force that was—for some reason—racially imbalanced, could be haled into court and forced to engage in the expensive and time-consuming task of defending the "business necessity" of the methods used to select the other members of his work force. The only practicable option for many employers will be to adopt racial quotas, insuring that no portion of his work force deviates in racial composition from the other portions thereof; this is a result that Congress expressly rejected in drafting Title VII.[122]

Moreover, the Court held, plaintiffs may not challenge the statistical "bottom line" of a range of employment practices, but must focus on the specific employment practices that produced the adverse impact. A converse rule, the Court observed, "would result in employers being potentially liable for 'the myriad of innocent causes that may lead to statistical imbalances in the composition of their work forces.'"[123] In other words, the employer in a purely statistical challenge cannot be forced to defend every single one of its employment practices, but only those that are identified as potentially discriminatory.

The Court then turned to the employer's burden once a *prima facie* showing is made, a burden the Court characterized not as one of proof but of "producing evidence of a business justification," since, as the Court noted, the "burden of persuasion ... remains with the disparate-impact plaintiff."[124] The Court emphasized that such evidence need show only that the "challenged practice serves, in a significant way, the legitimate employment goals of the employer," rather than that the practice is "essential" or "indispensable," since the latter standard "would be almost impossible for most employers to meet."[125] Plaintiffs would remain free to rebut such evidence by showing that alternative practices exist that would equally serve the employer's objectives, which would suggest the employer's justifications were pretextual.[126]

Atonio thus leaves intact adverse impact as a method of proving discrimination, but requires that the statistics presented actually raise a plausible inference of discrimination. The decision also raise a plausible inference of discrimination. The decision also serves the purposes of Title VII by preserving employer discretion with respect to nondiscriminatory employment practices.

Perhaps the decision will encourage as well new approaches that expand opportunities for minorities and focus on economic mobility and human capital development rather than quotas.[127] Stripped of its outcomes-oriented veneer, adverse impact can also take its place among principled methods by which to challenge arbitrary and discriminatory barriers to opportunity, such as occupational licensing requirements and restrictive zoning ordinances.*

Atonio creates significant opportunities to advance through litigation the traditional principles of civil rights. First and foremost, it allows employers to defend in a principled way their nondiscriminatory employment policies. Moreover, government policies based on misapplications of adverse impact—such as Executive Order 11246 and the EEOC Guidelines—are vulnerable to legal challenge.

One potentially fruitful litigation target is the practice of "race norming" imposed on state employment services by the United States Employment Service. The employment services give potential job candidates the General Aptitude Test Battery (GATB) and refer them in rank order to potential employers. The federal government insists the GATB is a good predictor of job performance. But since the test produces adverse impact, the government adjusts the scores for certain minority candidates to provide for racially proportional job referrals.[128] This blatant racial quota policy was always vulnerable to constitutional challenge, but it is now even more so since its theoretical foundation was seriously weakened by *Atonio*.

Nonetheless, such opportunities may be fleeting. The *Atonio* decision can be overturned by legislation, and bills to do just that are already pending.[129] The case must forcefully be made in the court of public opinion that a return to adverse impact as construed before *Atonio* means quotas—a step Congress has con-

---

*Unlike Title VII, plaintiffs in the context of the Fourteenth Amendment must establish an intent to discriminate in order to establish a constitutional violation. Adverse impact is one type of evidence, if buttressed by other evidence, by which discriminatory intent can be proved. See, e.g., *Village of Arlington Heights* v. *Metropolitan Housing Development Corp.*, 429 U.S. 252 (1977).

sistently refused to take—and that far preferable alternatives are available to expand opportunities for the economically disadvantaged. If that battle is lost, we will suffer a major setback in the quest for equality under law.

Equal Educational Opportunities

In terms of oppressive barriers to opportunity and individual autonomy, none of the legacies of *Plessy* was more debilitating than school segregation. But although we have made enormous progress in the years following *Brown* in eradicating school segregation, we have accomplished precious little in securing the real goal of *Brown*: equal educational opportunities for minority schoolchildren.

This sobering reality confirms the inadequacy of race-based remedies in addressing the needs of the economically disadvantaged. As Charles Murray reports, "As of 1980, the gap in educational achievement between black and white students was so great that it threatened to defeat any other attempts to narrow the economic differences separating blacks and whites."[130] That gap has not narrowed since 1980.

The failure to make progress in expanding educational opportunities is largely attributable to the civil rights establishment's substitution of the goals of opportunity and individual autonomy for the goal of racial balancing, effectuated primarily through forced busing. As columnist William Raspberry describes it, the civil rights leadership elite is today "almost monomaniacally concerned with the maximum feasible mixing of races, with educational concerns a distant second."[131] This changed emphasis is reflected in a series of Supreme Court decisions after *Brown* that make racial balancing the key factor in determining the accomplishment of desegregation.[132]

As a consequence, some school districts that have long since eradicated discriminatory barriers are entering their third decade of judicial control in a never-ending, never-attainable effort to attain perfect racial balance. Meanwhile, middle-class white and black students are fleeing the urban public school systems; are opting for private and suburban public schools; and are leaving behind the disintegrated public schools beset by drugs, violence, bureaucratic incompetence, and unrestrained social engineering.

As in the case of Mark Anthony Nevels, these issues often pit the interests of individual parents against the ideological agenda of the civil rights leadership elite. Increasingly, minority parents, whose children bear the greatest burden of busing orders and who often have no alternative but the public schools, are breaking ranks with the civil rights establishment and demanding an end to forced busing. In Denver, some of the original desegregation plaintiffs joined the school board's unsuccessful petition to restore community control of the schools after nearly two decades of court control.[133] Nathan Glazer summarizes the irony of the situation:

> Constitutional law often moves along strange and circuitous paths, but perhaps the strangest yet has been the one whereby, beginning with an effort to expand freedom—no black child shall be excluded from any public school because of his race—the law has ended up with as drastic a restriction of freedom as we have seen in this country in recent years: No child, of any race or group, may "escape" or "flee" the school to which that child has been assigned on the basis of his or her race.[134]

These excesses in the name of desegregation provide important litigation opportunities, both in curtailing those excesses and in moving forward in the quest for equal educational opportunities.

The first area is a likely candidate for substantial attention in the near future by the Supreme Court.* As school districts move toward "unitariness"—that is, eradication from their school systems of the previously "dual" (segregated) elements—controversies are arising over the showing necessary to attain such status and the significance of the status once attained. Despite the common understanding that busing was a temporary, extraordinary remedial device, civil rights establishment groups in case after case are betraying their true motivations by insisting that school districts retain busing even after attaining unitary status—in other words, permanent busing. In doing so, they are distancing themselves from the best interests of their supposed constituents, many of whom surely would prefer that their school

---

*As this book was entering publication, the Supreme Court decided to consider this issue in *Oklahoma City Board of Education* v. *Dowell,* which is discussed later in this section.

systems focus on educational opportunities rather than racial balancing.

The Supreme Court has not visited the desegregation issue for several years, during which time the composition of the Court has significantly changed. Even before that time, however, the Court was beginning to set limits on desegregation decrees on the basis of the equitable principle that a judicially imposed remedy may not exceed the scope of the constitutional violation. In *Milliken* v. *Bradley*,[135] for instance, the Court ruled that busing orders could not exceed school district boundaries in most circumstances. And in *Spangler* v. *Pasadena City Board of Education*,[136] the Court held that a school system that had not yet attained unitary status could not be required to readjust its attendance zones to account for demographic changes.

A split among the federal circuit courts has developed over issues relating to unitary status. In its 1986 *Dowell* decision, the Tenth Circuit ruled that "the purpose of court-ordered school integration is not only to achieve, but also to *maintain*, a unitary school system."[137] Accordingly, the court invalidated a unitary school district's plan to dismantle part of its busing program, even though the district would have provided free transportation for those students who wished to transfer to schools in which they would be in the minority (e.g., black students transferring to predominantly white schools). Conversely, the Fifth Circuit ruled in *United States* v. *Overton*[138] that once a school district is unitary, plaintiffs may challenge school district policies only by establishing a new constitutional violation on the basis of proof of discriminatory intent. In *Overton*, Judge Patrick Higginbotham explained that the "difficulty with *Dowell*'s approach is that it denies meaning to unitariness by failing ever to end judicial superintendence of the schools,"[139] in essence constituting "a heady call for raw judicial power."[140]

These issues—wresting control of the schools from the clutches of the judiciary and returning power to the community and individual parents—provide an excellent chance to assert the interests of disadvantaged plaintiffs and to restore the quest for equal educational opportunities to its original course.

Likewise, desegregation cases offer enormous potential to expand educational liberty. Particularly in cases where courts have for years deployed, without success, coercive measures to secure equal educational opportunities, minority plaintiffs could demand monetary damages instead—in essence, a "voucher" remedy.[141] The plaintiffs would point to the futility of busing mechanisms in securing equal educational opportunities, they would show that well-integrated urban private schools (and/or suburban public schools) were willing and able to provide such opportunities, and they would ask for their *pro rata* share of public educational expenditures in order to avail themselves of those opportunities. Such a strategy would at once vindicate the principles of equal protection—in a manner far more effective, yet far less divisive, than busing remedies—while empowering individuals to choose among educational alternatives, thereby expanding educational opportunities for those who need them the most.[142]

The first test case of this empowerment strategy was filed recently in the midst of the Kansas City desegregation quagmire; it seeks monetary damages to allow individual parents to select the best education for their children.[143] The Supreme Court's recent decision in *Martin* v. *Wilks* may open the door for such plaintiffs to argue that their rights should not be foreclosed by prior litigation. A voucher remedy to allow youngsters to opt out of the public school monopoly is also viable in other contexts, such as to redress violations of religious liberty[144] or of state statutory guarantees of public school safety or competency.

The public school monopoly holds hostage the dreams and aspirations of poor and minority children throughout the nation. Litigation efforts to free schoolchildren from these shackles would make an enormous contribution to the ability of individuals to control their own destinies.

FUTURE DIRECTIONS

Even outside the context of race-related issues, current equal protection jurisprudence provides an important battleground for the competing visions of civil rights.

The civil rights revisionists are eager to use the equal protection clause to ensure equality of results by expanding the list of "suspect" classifications and by protecting entitlements in the guise of fundamental rights. The newest innovation is an assault on "poverty discrimination." As Julius L. Chambers, director-counsel of the NAACP Legal Defense and Educational Fund, Inc., describes it, this theory would

> establish constitutional protection against disparate treatment of the poor based on their economic status. This is an area of emerging constitutional law that will have tremendous impact on civil rights. Just as *Brown* took aim at the "separate-but-equal" doctrine embodied in *Plessy*, today the target is a 1973 Supreme Court decision, *San Antonio* v. *Rodriguez*, which held that it was not a violation of the Constitution for the state of Texas to allow unequal funding among school districts based on the economic status of the districts or the students residing in the districts.[145]

Such a theory combines adverse impact violations with mandated equal outcome relief in cases involving public services. Though a majority of the Supreme Court recently rejected such a theory,[146] it commanded the support of two justices, Thurgood Marshall and William Brennan. Condemning the majority for upholding a statute that allowed certain school districts to charge a user fee for school bus transportation, Justice Marshall reasoned that the fee "discriminated against [plaintiff's] family because it necessarily fell more heavily upon the poor than upon wealthier members of the community"[!],[147] leading Marshall to proclaim that "I do not believe that this Court should sanction discrimination against the poor."[148] Though this theory's proponents presently do not command majority support on the Supreme Court, they doubtlessly will pursue the theory in state courts.

Meanwhile, advocates of liberty have an opportunity to secure greater judicial scrutiny for unjust, arbitrary, or irrational classifications by which government allocates rights and privileges. In its decision in *Cleburne*, the Court signaled a willingness to look behind governmental classifications to ensure they are legitimate, rather than attempts to use the coercive power of government to benefit some and to burden others. As noted in Part 2, other courts have followed the Supreme Court's lead in

Cleburne, thereby making the equal protection clause a much more viable safeguard against governmental oppression.

Litigation strategies designed to make good on the promise of equality under law can effectively be combined with efforts to protect fundamental rights, such as economic liberty, as both the Ego Brown and Alfredo Santos cases illustrate. A civil rights challenge to the Davis-Bacon Act, for instance, would provide an excellent example. Davis-Bacon was instigated by labor unions seeking to gain a competitive advantage in public works contracts, through a requirement that such contracts must provide for "prevailing wages." The law is classic protectionist legislation, through which the unions use the power of government to redistribute opportunities for their benefit. Moreover, the law was explicitly motivated by the desire to exclude blacks from the construction trades. Consequently, the law violates both the principle of equality under law and the fundamental right of economic liberty. As is often the case, the two approaches complement and enhance one another.

For more than a century, the courts have thwarted the intent of the equal protection clause. Most recently, the courts have allowed government at every level to use its coercive power to redistribute rights and opportunities, with the courts often using the equal protection clause and civil rights statutes not to protect against such abuses, but to facilitate them. Every departure from the principle of equality under law has imposed tremendous costs on individual liberty.

The equal protection clause is at once not nearly so potent as to solve every problem of society, yet it is far too important to allow its sacrifice in the cause of unbridled social engineering. A movement whose mission is the empowerment of individuals must insist upon judicial fidelity to and enforcement of the Constitution's guarantee of equal protection of the laws. Efforts to finally and forever overturn the pernicious doctrine of *Plessy* v. *Ferguson*, and thereby to vindicate the core values of the equal protection clause, will move us toward completing a great objective of the quest for civil rights: the promise of equality under law for all Americans.

ENDNOTES

1. Paine, *Dissertation*, p. 200.
2. *Cong. Globe*, 39th Cong., 1st Sess., 1866, S. p. 344.
3. Landmark Legal Foundation is challenging this policy on behalf of Demond Crawford, Mary Amaya, and several other black schoolchildren and their parents in *Crawford* v. *Honig*, no. C–89–0014–RFP (N.D. Cal., filed 20 May 1988).
4. *The Federalist*, no. 10 (Madison).
5. Macey, p. 243.
6. *Id.*, p. 249.
7. See *The Federalist*, no. 78 (Hamilton).
8. Cass Sunstein, "Naked Preferences and the Constitution," 84 *Colum. L. Rev.* 1689, 1689 (1984).
9. Paine, "A Serious Address to the People of Pennsylvania." In Dishman, p. 198 note 2.
10. *Cong. Globe*, 39th Cong., 1st Sess., 1866, S. p. 2765.
11. *Id.*, p. 65.
12. *Cong. Globe*, 43rd Cong., 1st Sess., 1874, H. p. 413.
13. *Cong. Globe*, 39th Cong., 1st Sess., 1866, S. p. 343.
14. Quoted in Eastland and Bennett, p. 62.
15. *City of Cleburne* v. *Cleburne Living Center*, 473 U.S. 432, 439 (1985).
16. See, e.g., Karlin, p. 659.
17. Lofgren, p. 9.
18. *Id.*, pp. 17–18.
19. *Id.*, p. 32.
20. *Plessy*, p. 544.
21. *Id.*, pp. 544–46.
22. *Id.*, p. 550.
23. *Id.*, p. 563 (Harlan, J., dissenting).
24. *Id.*, p. 559.
25. *Berea College* v. *Kentucky*, 211 U.S. 45, 67 (Harlan, J., dissenting).
26. *Id.*, p. 69.
27. Lofgren, p. 92.
28. *Korematsu* v. *United States*, 323 U.S. 214 (1944).
29. *Id.*, pp. 245–46 (Jackson, J., dissenting).
30. Bolick, *Changing Course*, p. 65.
31. Robert Pear, "Civil Rights Agency Splits in Debate on Narrowing

Definition of Equality," *New York Times*, 14 October 1985, p. A17.

32. Benjamin L. Hooks, "The U.S. Constitution Was Never Color–Blind," *New York Times*, 27 November 1985, p. A22.
33. Quoted in Allen, p. 44.
34. *Brown*, p. 493.
35. *Id.*, pp. 492–93.
36. *Id.*, pp. 493–95.
37. *Id.*, p. 495.
38. Lofgren, p. 204.
39. W. B. Allen, *A New Birth of Freedom: Fulfillment or Derailment?* (Washington, American Enterprise Institute, 1985), p. 41.
40. *Id.*, pp. 42–43.
41. *Legislative History of Titles VII and XI of the Civil Rights Act of 1964* (Washington: United States Equal Employment Opportunity Commission, undated), p. 3187.
42. 110 *Cong. Rec.* 5423 (1964).
43. Quoted in Eastland and Bennett, p. 207.
44. *Id.*, p. 3015.
45. *Id.*
46. Glazer, p. 31.
47. Abram, p. 1321.
48. DuBois, p. 13.
49. Eleanor Holmes Norton, "Equal Employment Law: Crisis in Interpretation—Survival Against the Odds," 62 *Tul. L. Rev.* 681, 696 (1988).
50. I am indebted to Jeremy Rabkin for this metaphor.
51. *DeFunis* v. *Odegaard*, p. 343 (Douglas, J., dissenting).
52. *Regents of The University of California* v. *Bakke*, 438 U.S. 265 (1978).
53. *Id.*, pp. 289–90 (Opinion of Powell, J.).
54. *Id.*, pp. 290–91.
55. *Id.*, pp. 294–95.
56. *Id.*, pp. 311–20.
57. *Id.*, pp. 373–74 (Brennan, J., concurring in the judgment in part and dissenting in part).
58. *Id.*, p. 336.
59. *Id.*, p. 339.
60. *Id.*, p. 362.
61. *Id.*, p. 357.
62. *Id.*, p. 407 (Opinion of Blackmun, J.).

63. *Marsh* v. *Bd. of Educ. of City of Flint*, 581 F.Supp. 614, 623 (E.D. Mich. 1984), *aff'd mem.*, 762 F.2d 1009 (6th Cir. 1985), *cert. granted and remanded*, 476 U.S. 1137 (1986).

64. *Id.*, p. 401 (Opinion of Marshall, J.).

65. Excellent summaries of the cases during this period are provided in William Bradford Reynolds, "An Equal Opportunity Scorecard," 21 *Ga. L. Rev.* 1007 (1987); and in Detlefsen, pp. 75–132.

66. *Fullilove* v. *Klutznick*, 448 U.S. 448 (1980).

67. *United Steelworkers* v. *Weber*, 443 U.S. 193 (1979).

68. *Local 28, Sheet Metal Workers* v. *EEOC*, 478 U.S. 421 (1986).

69. *United States* v. *Paradise*, 480 U.S. 149 (1987).

70. *Johnson* v. *Transportation Agency*, 480 U.S. 616 (1987).

71. *Firefighters Local Union No. 1784* v. *Stotts*, 467 U.S. 561 (1984).

72. *Wygant* v. *Jackson Board of Education*, 476 U.S. 267 (1986).

73. See, e.g., *Bratton* v. *City of Detroit*, 704 F.2d 878 (6th Cir. 1983), *cert. denied*, 464 U.S. 1040 (1984).

74. *City of Richmond* v. *J. A. Croson Co.*, 109 S.Ct. 706 (1989).

75. *Id.*, p. 727.

76. *Id.*, p. 728.

77. *Id.*, p. 724.

78. *Id.*, p. 727.

79. *Id.*, p. 728.

80. *Id.*, p. 735 (Scalia, J., concurring in the judgment).

81. *Id.*, p. 739, referring to the plaintiffs in the *DeFunis* and *Johnson* cases cited above.

82. *Id.*, p. 737 (citation omitted).

83. *Id.*, p. 735.

84. *Id.*, p. 739.

85. *Id.*

86. *Id.*, p. 734 (Kennedy, J., concurring in part and concurring in the judgment).

87. *Id.*

88. *Hammon* v. *Barry*, 813 F.2d 412 (D.C. Cir. 1987), *cert. denied*, 108 S.Ct. 2023 (1988); *Michigan Road Builders Ass'n* v. *Milliken*, 834 F.2d 583 (6th Cir. 1987); *Britton* v. *South Bend Community School Corp.*, 819 F.2d 766 (7th Cir.)(*en banc*), *cert. denied*, 108 S.Ct. 288 (1987); *Assoc. Gen. Contractors* v. *City and County of San Francisco*, 813 F.2d 922 (9th Cir. 1987).

89. *Martin* v. *Wilks*, 109 S.Ct. 2180 (1989).

90. See John H. Bunzel, "Affirmative–Action Admissions: How It 'Works' at UC Berkeley," 93 *The Public Interest* 111 (1988); James

S. Gibney, "The Berkeley Squeeze," *The New Republic*, 11 April 1988, p. 15.

91. See, e.g., *United States* v. *Starrett City Assocs.*, 660 F.Supp. 668 (E.D.N.Y. 1987), *aff'd*, 840 F.2d 1096 (2d Cir.), *cert. denied*, 109 S.Ct. 376 (1988).

92. *Griggs* v. *Duke Power Co.*, 401 U.S. 424 (1971).

93. Earl M. Maltz, "The Expansion of the Role of the Effects Test in Antidiscrimination Law: A Critical Analysis," 59 *Neb. L. Rev.* 345, 345 (1980).

94. Norton, p. 692 n. 44 [emphasis added].

95. *Id.*, p. 696.

96. *Griggs*, p. 426.

97. *Id.*, p. 436.

98. *Id.*, p. 430.

99. *Id.*, p. 431.

100. See, e.g., the opinion of Judge Richard Posner concurring in part and dissenting in part in *United States* v. *Town of Cicero*, 786 F.2d 331 (7th Cir. 1986).

101. *International Brotherhood of Teamsters* v. *United States*, 431 U.S. 324, 340 n. 20 (1977).

102. See, e.g., Thomas Sowell, *Civil Rights: Rhetoric or Reality?* (New York: William Morrow and Co., 1984), pp. 53–56.

103. See Barbara Lindeman Schlei and Paul Grossman, *Employment Discrimination Law*, 2d ed. (Washington: Bureau of National Affairs, Inc., 1988), pp. 1324–25.

104. 29 C.F.R., section 1607.

105. *Watkins* v. *Scott Paper Co.*, 530 F.2d 1159, 1168 (5th Cir. 1976), *cert. denied*, 429 U.S. 861 (1976).

106. *United States* v. *Bethlehem Steel Corp.*, 446 F.2d 652, 662 (2d Cir. 1971).

107. Michael Gold, "*Griggs'* Folly: An Essay on the Theory, Problems, and Origin of the Adverse Impact Definition of Employment Discrimination and a Recommendation for Reform," 7 *Indus. Rel. L. J.* 429, 460 (1985).

108. *United States* v. *Georgia Power Co.*, 3 Fair Empl. Prac. Cas. (BNA) 767, 780 (N.D. Ga.), *rev'd*, 474 F.2d 906 (5th Cir. 1973).

109. *Albemarle Paper Co.* v. *Moody*, 422 U.S. 405, 449 (1975) (Blackmun, J., concurring in the judgment).

110. Gold, p. 457.

111. Edward E. Potter, ed., *Employee Selection: Legal and Practical Alternatives to Compliance and Litigation*, 2d ed. (Washington:

National Foundation for the Study of Equal Employment Policy, 1986), p. 215.

112. Maltz, p. 353; Potter, pp. 315–19.

113. Quoted in Bolick, *Changing Course*, p. 63.

114. See, e.g., Wilson, p. 110.

115. Maltz, p. 362.

116. For a brilliant analysis of the adoption of adverse impact in the voting rights area, see Abigail Thernstrom, *Whose Votes Count? Affirmative Action and Minority Voting Rights* (Cambridge: Harvard University Press, 1987).

117. See, e.g., *United States* v. *City of Black Jack*, 508 F.2d 1179 (8th Cir. 1974), *cert. denied*, 422 U.S. 1042 (1975).

118. See Clint Bolick, "The Age Discrimination in Employment Act: Equal Opportunity or Reverse Discrimination?" *Policy Analysis* no. 82 (Washington: Cato Institute, 1987).

119. *Wards Cove Packing Co.* v. *Atonio*, 109 S.Ct. 2115 (1989).

120. *Id.*, p. 2117.

121. *Id.*, p. 2122 [citation omitted].

122. *Id.*

123. *Id.*, p. 2125 [citation omitted].

124. *Id.*, p. 2126.

125. *Id.*, pp. 2125–26 [citation omitted].

126. *Id.*, p. 2126.

127. See Bolick and Nestleroth.

128. See Clint Bolick, "Legal and Policy Aspects of Testing," 33 *J. of Vocational Behavior* 320 (1988): 325–27.

129. Principal among them are s.2104 (Kennedy) and H4000 (Hawkins), introduced in February 1990.

130. Charles Murray, *Losing Ground* (New York: Basic Books, Inc., 1984), p. 105.

131. William Raspberry, "The Easy Answer: Busing," *Washington Post*, 10 April 1985, p. A23.

132. See Bolick, *Changing Course*, pp. 60–63.

133. *Id.*, pp. 61–63.

134. Glazer, pp. 109–10.

135. *Milliken* v. *Bradley*, 418 U.S. 717 (1974).

136. *Spangler* v. *Pasadena Board of Education*, 427 U.S. 424 (1976).

137. *Dowell* v. *Bd. of Educ. of the Oklahoma City Public Schools, Indep. Dist. No. 89*, 795 F.2d 1516, 1520 (10th Cir. 1986).

138. *United States* v. *Overton*, 834 F.2d 1171 (5th Cir. 1987).

139. *Id.*, p. 1175.

140. *Id.*, p. 1176.
141. I am indebted to Jack Coons, professor of law at the University of California, for sharing this theory with me.
142. See Bolick, *Changing Course*, pp. 104–12.
143. *Rivarde* v. *School Dist. of Kansas City, Mo.*, No. 89–0671–CW8 (W.D. Mo., filed 14 July 1989).
144. See, e.g., *Mozert* v. *Hawkins County Bd. of Educ.*, 827 F.2d 1058 (6th Cir. 1987) (overturning such a remedy on the grounds that no constitutional violation occurred).
145. Julius L. Chambers, "What Color IS the Constitution?" *Human Rights* (Fall 1988): 45–47, citing *San Antonio* v. *Rodriguez*, 411 U.S. 1 (1973).
146. *Kadrmas* v. *Dickinson Public Schools*, 108 S.Ct. 2481 (1988).
147. *Id.*, p. 2492 (Marshall, J., dissenting).
148. *Id.*, p. 2491.

Part IV

TACTICAL CONSIDERATIONS AND CONCLUDING OBSERVATIONS

I have in the preceding pages outlined a strategy that I believe can help us fulfill at long last our nation's doctrinal commitment to civil rights. These concluding observations relate to the overall strategy, particularly by way of trying to anticipate possible objections and to respond to them at the outset.

The strategy I have presented is at once both modest and ambitious. Modest because it requires no new statutes or constitutional amendments, only that we enforce those that are on the books. The strategy is ambitious because we are far from that objective, which we can accomplish only by altering the course of more than a century of jurisprudence.

Isn't it dangerous, one might ask, to reveal this strategy in advance for the world to see? This concern has certainly occurred to me, but I conclude that the benefits outweigh the risks. When the architects of the NAACP's legal struggle to overturn "separate but equal" launched their enterprise early in this century, they were fairly straightforward about their motives and strategy. Such an approach was warranted, I believe, by at least four factors that are equally applicable to the endeavor proposed here. First, any legal theory or strategy benefits from criticism, which allows its proponents to modify or refine it and thereby to strengthen it. Second, the enterprise is not subversive. It does not seek to distort any constitutional provision or to promote any special interest. Rather, it seeks to give full meaning to constitutional provisions whose own framers characterized as akin to a Magna Charta. Third, as a tactical matter, the strategy is an evolutionary one. It builds upon existing precedent, each case laying the foundation to secure for all individuals the full range of rights contemplated by our system of government. Finally, the enterprise is moral. It appeals to and rests upon the very principles on which our nation's moral claim is staked. For all these reasons, I do not think we have much to fear from setting forth our goals and the methods by which we intend to achieve them.

Why is this strategy addressed to the courts? Quite frankly, I would prefer that civil rights receive full protection from the executive and legislative branches of government. And indeed, as I noted in my introductory remarks, a legal strategy is necessarily only one part of a broader empowerment strategy that includes legislative and executive initiatives as well as individual self-help. But as our nation's founders recognized, the legislative and executive branches are especially susceptible to majoritarian and special interest influences. Since civil rights are by definition individual rights—asserted either against other individuals or the government itself—the ultimate guardian of those rights, when the other branches of government have failed adequately to protect them, is the judiciary. I recognize how imperfectly the judiciary has provided that protection to date, and indeed that the judiciary all too often violates rather than safeguards those rights. But these considerations, it seems to me, speak in favor of increasing our activities in the courts rather than diminishing them.

I noted that the strategy outlined here builds upon, rather than breaks from, recent precedents. This applies as well to the overall policy direction proposed. I have argued that much recent civil rights policy has strayed from the core principles of civil rights as traditionally defined by their greatest American proponents, and that a new direction conforming to those principles is necessary. I want to emphasize, however, that such a change in direction assumes, and in fact depends upon, the vigorous enforcement of constitutional and statutory protections of civil rights. That much should be quite implicit in all I have written, but too often the debate over recent civil rights policies is perceived as a debate over whether we should have civil rights at all. Those who would in any sense "turn back the clock" on basic civil rights protections will find no refuge in a strategy of individual empowerment; quite the contrary, those who oppose civil rights ought to prefer the current policies that pit American against American in a battle over entitlements.

The point I have just made bears repeating: the essential foundation of a forward-looking empowerment strategy is the vigorous enforcement of existing civil rights protections. While our adversaries look backward, we must look forward. Let others cling in reactionary fashion to the failed agenda of social engineering built from the cloth of *Plessy* v. *Ferguson,* while we tend to the real civil rights problems of the 1990s and beyond.

This brings me to my final point. Those who have resisted the civil rights policies of the past quarter century have been accused, often justly, of offering no alternative. The lack of a coherent, credible, and comprehensive alternative leaves us in the untenable posture of arguing either that all of our nation's civil rights problems have been solved or that the major civil rights issue of our era is the plight of white firefighters victimized by reverse discrimination. If that is our response, our detractors may be excused for calling into question our commitment to civil rights.

No, our strategy must recognize that we have yet a distance to travel before all Americans are secure in their civil rights. For so long as victims of official discrimination exist; for so long as people like Ego Brown and Mark Anthony Nevels and Demond Crawford and Alfredo Santos are denied basic freedoms and equality under law, we have much work to do.

It is far easier to criticize and condemn than to offer a viable solution. The latter is what I have attempted here.

Unlike those policies I hope an empowerment strategy will supplant, I do not claim that such a strategy will ensure harmony or prosperity. Even if all the objectives of an empowerment strategy were accomplished overnight, it would not—indeed could not—deliver equality of results.

An empowerment strategy is far more ambitious than that. It promises freedom.

We can vindicate the architects of the great American experiment only through a passionate commitment to the principles of liberty. I hope this book provides a practical framework for those with the requisite passion to begin moving in the right direction.

Appendix 1

TEN COMMANDMENTS FOR A SUCCESSFUL PUBLIC INTEREST LITIGATION STRATEGY

I have often joked to friends that what I do for a living is "ambulance chasing," much like those personal injury lawyers who roam the countryside looking for potential lawsuits. I only wish my version of this practice were nearly so lucrative!

Though an oversimplification, that analogy is not terribly wide of the mark in describing the type of skills a public interest litigator must possess: a good eye for the right cases and clients, a good imagination, and an ability to persuasively argue novel legal theories. I have often consoled law clerks who were disconcerted over not finding voluminous precedential support for our arguments by reminding them that if the law was where we wanted it to be, we wouldn't be in business.

An advocate for liberty in the courts needs additional skills as well. First and foremost, he or she must possess a deep understanding of and passion for the principles involved, and a good idea of how to advance those principles through litigation.

During my seven years as an attorney, I have had significant opportunities to observe what works and doesn't work in public interest litigation. I have participated in the conservative public interest law community, which has had more than its share of failures but a few notable achievements.* And I have studied the remarkable successes of left-wing advocacy organizations such as the NAACP Legal Defense and Education Fund, Inc. From these experiences I have derived several rules of thumb that I believe will have a great impact on the success of a public interest litigation program, which are as follows:

1. *Articulate Clearly Defined Long-Range Goals.* No coherent litigation strategy can be crafted without a clear understanding of the ultimate objectives, namely, vindicating the underlying principles and achieving the desired long-range change in the law. Once the principles are articulated and the long-range goals are established, every individual case should be measured against those principles and goals to keep the program on course. Otherwise, the public interest law firm is just another law firm, out to win cases but not making much progress or advancing principles in any methodical way.

2. *Focus on Direct Litigation in Federal Courts.* Some organizations file very few lawsuits and instead concentrate their resources on producing *amicus curiae* ("friend of the court") briefs. Though *amicus* briefs sometimes have marginal value, particularly in lower courts where they are not as common, they are almost never a cost-effective investment in terms of affecting the law. Only through direct litigation can a public interest lawyer frame the issues, control the record, or have any serious influence on the ultimate outcome. Direct litigation is expensive and time-consuming, but it is the only way to make a real difference. Moreover, litigation strategies should focus on the federal courts, at least initially when resources are scarce. Federal court decisions have greater precedential value, particularly with respect to federal constitutional issues; the litigator can make state law arguments under the federal courts' pendent jurisdiction.

Additionally, public interest firms should engage in creative

---

*Pacific Legal Foundation's strategy in the private property rights area, leading to its smashing victory in *Nollan* v. *California Coastal Comm'n*, 483 U.S. 825 (1987), exemplifies the type of creative, tenacious, principled, and skillful effort required for successful public interest litigation.

intervention in lawsuits filed by their adversaries. Often named defendants in such lawsuits are corporations or other entities that are not accustomed to making principled "public interest" arguments. Intervention in such lawsuits by public interest groups, typically representing third parties (such as consumers, shareholders, taxpayers, employees, parents, etc.) whose interests are at stake, can improve the odds substantially.*

3. *Develop a Systematic Point-by-Point Strategy.* Successful implementation of a long-range agenda requires assessing where incremental gains can be scored and directing the litigation accordingly. Each successive case should be viewed as a building block, starting with the point at which existing law is most vulnerable. Such a strategy allows the lawyer to shop around for cases that fit the bill, and to gear them to sympathetic judicial forums. Even defeats can advance the strategy by creating splits among jurisdictions (thus increasing the odds of Supreme Court review), by providing guidance in fine-tuning strategy, and by creating public support that may translate into future triumphs.

4. *Find Sympathetic Plaintiffs.* A white firefighter who loses a promotion because of a racial quota and a black schoolchild who is turned away from a magnet school in order to preserve racial balance are fighting for precisely the same principle. But one scenario provides a more sympathetic plaintiff with which to advance that principle. Given limited resources, public interest litigators should represent the most disadvantaged individuals and should try wherever possible to find a plaintiff whose plight outrages people.

5. *Present Unblemished Facts.* The old litigator's maxim "If you don't have the facts, argue the law; if you don't have the law, argue the facts" holds especially true for public interest litigation. No excuse exists for anything less than a pristine factual scenario. The other side must be reduced to arguing

---

*In a previous practice, I represented a group of female prison guards as intervenors/defendants in a "comparable worth" lawsuit filed against the State of Illinois. These women were employed in a male-dominated job classification and would suffer adverse consequences as a result if comparable worth were implemented. Their presence in the lawsuit helped defuse the notion that salary differences among various job classifications had anything to do with sex discrimination.

cold, hard legal precedent; the angels should always be in court on the side of the public interest advocate.

6. *Find Cases Amenable to Summary Judgment.* The ideal case is one that delivers bang for the buck, and factually uncomplicated cases tend to maximize the former and minimize the latter. Prosecuting factually "clean" cases not only reduces costs thereby allowing the public interest firm to litigate more cases, but also makes more likely resolution of the cases on the basis of principles rather than factual quirks.

7. *Generate Scholarly Support.* Careful coordination with supporters in the academic and public policy communities is essential to success. Legal pioneers are well-served by capable advance scouts, who blaze the trails with sound and creative jurisprudential scholarship. Law review articles and other scholarly publications supporting and developing novel legal theories provide a strong foundation for pathbreaking litigation.

8. *Argue the Case in the Court of Public Opinion.* A good public interest case is often an attractive news story. Public opinion sometimes drives judicial outcomes, and it certainly encourages legislative reforms. Moreover, the arena of public opinion offers a good sounding board for a litigator: if he or she can make a compelling argument to the public, that same argument can often translate extremely well into the courtroom. Cases should thus be viewed in part as "teaching vehicles" by which to inform the public as well as the courts.

9. *Generate Amicus Support.* Although *amicus* briefs are often not seriously considered by courts, such briefs can demonstrate public support, can lend a mainstream imprimatur to a novel argument, or can underscore the importance of an issue. They are often most helpful if the *amicus* is a group with a different philosophical view or a recognized expertise on a particular issue. Groups with widely divergent views can sometimes reach common cause on a particular issue, a tactic that offers strategic advantages so long as the litigating organization remains true to its principles.

10. *Separate Fundraising from the Case Selection Function.* Coming full circle back to the primary importance of principled long-range goals, it is absolutely essential that groups ded-

to such goals understand the respective roles of fundraising and case selection. Funds are raised to support the cases—not vice-versa. This rule is critical not only for the organization's integrity, but also for the mission's success. While no public interest group can afford to overlook funding realities, allowing such concerns to dictate or heavily influence case selection confuses ends with means. An organization that takes a practical yet principled approach should over the long run find that a funding base oriented toward principles is much more stable and supportive than one geared toward specific outcomes.

The key to success in any public interest litigation program is an unyielding commitment to principles. Too often, public interest law firms have lost sight of their original goals, ultimately viewing the perpetuation of their particular programs as ends in themselves and engaging in mercenary tactics to advance their programs even at the cost of the very principles that are their reason for existence. Such organizations not only are worthless, they detract from those who are sincerely committed to principles by diverting scarce resources and by fostering cynicism about the entire movement.

In any event, any short-term gains that might temporarily accrue from compromising principles are vastly outweighed by the rewards that can result from a steadfast devotion to principle. Imagine how James Meredith's lawyers must have felt when they watched him walk through the doors of the University of Mississippi or how Thurgood Marshall must have felt when he saw black and white schoolchildren sitting side by side in Topeka, Kansas. From my own experience, I can attest to the enormous personal satisfaction I felt when I saw Ego Brown back on the streets of Washington, once again earning a living in his chosen profession and giving shoes a "touch of class"—a man restored of his spirit, his ambitions, his dignity.

Law can be a mighty tool. In the hands of a skilled and principled practitioner, it can be a powerful weapon in the arsenal of liberty. It is time for the defenders of freedom to take to the courtrooms and join the battle on our terms.

Appendix 2

LITIGATION PROTOTYPES

Landmark Legal Foundation and its Center for Civil Rights recently have filed a number of cases that provide good examples of innovative, forward-looking litigation in the areas of economic liberty and equality under law. These cases illustrate how principles can be translated into concrete legal action as part of a comprehensive litigation strategy.

Economic Liberty Cases

Since March 1988, the Landmark Center for Civil Rights has filed three cases as part of a principled, long-range strategy to restore protection for economic liberty as a fundamental civil right.

In *Brown* v. *Barry*,[1] the Center challenged a barrier to the quintessentially entry-level entrepreneurial opportunity—street-corner shoeshining. Representing shoeshine artist Ego Brown and two homeless men he employed at his portable stands, the Center filed suit against a Jim Crow–era District of Columbia law that prohibited shoeshine stands on public space. The Center combined the Fourteenth Amendment economic liberty arguments outlined in Part 2 with evidence that the law was passed with racially discriminatory intent.

In an initial opinion denying a preliminary injunction on the grounds that no irreparable harm was shown, the district court embraced the Center's economic liberty arguments. The court applied the "rational basis" test, finding no justification for prohibiting shoeshine stands while permitting other forms of vending operations.[2] The court declared that "the right to follow a chosen profession free from *unreasonable* governmental interference has rightly been held to be protected under certain constitutional restraints" and that "the federal courts' role in protecting American citizens from unreasonable economic regulation has been one of the hallmarks of American liberty, prosperity, and progress."[3] The court concluded that the plaintiffs demonstrated a substantial likelihood of success on the merits.

In its final opinion on summary judgment, the court declared the law unconstitutional. The court stated that it had "no difficulty finding that the bootblack prohibition fails to pass the rational basis test,"[4] concluding that "we would have to 'strain our imagination' ... to justify prohibiting bootblacks from the use of public space while permitting access to virtually every other type of vendor."[5] The decision was not appealed.

The Ego Brown case was triumphant not only in the district court but also in the court of public opinion. Favorable articles appeared in the *Wall Street Journal, New York Times, Washington Post*, and other periodicals, and ABC-TV featured Brown as its "Person of the Week." The previously recalcitrant District of Columbia government adopted a proclamation establishing "Ego Brown Day" and commending Brown for his persistence and for his efforts to provide opportunities for homeless people. The success of the Ego Brown case illustrates that both judicial victories and public support can be achieved in the cause of economic liberty.

In *Santos* v. *City of Houston*,[6] the Center is challenging, on behalf of entrepreneur Alfredo Santos, the city's Anti-Jitney Law of 1924. A "jitney" is a cross between a bus and a taxicab, using a small vehicle and operating on a semi-fixed route for a flat fee. Jitneys were banned in most cities throughout the country early in this century to protect the streetcar industry from competition. Santos started a popular jitney service in the early 1980s to offer a transportation option to customers in low-income neighborhoods, but he quickly had his business shut down.

The Center is challenging the law on the Fourteenth Amendment grounds summarized above and as a violation of federal and state antitrust laws. As in *Brown*, the law is an anachronistic barrier to entry-level entrepreneurial opportunities; it singles out a specific type of business for adverse regulatory treatment. The case presently is submitted on cross-motions for summary judgment.

In *Allick* v. *Lujan*,[7] the Center is challenging, on behalf of a third-generation sea captain who is a native of the Virgin Islands, a National Park Service "attrition" policy that governs charter boat permits and that has destroyed a traditional native business. The Park Service initiated in 1979 a permit policy for charter boats to Buck Island, whose beautiful coral reef is a prime destination of choice for visitors to St. Croix. Concerned about "predatory price cutting" among boat operators, the Park Service reduced substantially the number of permit holders on the basis of minor technical violations (in Allick's case, keeping the boat out of commission longer than the permissible time for repairs). Over a 10-year period, all of the native Virgin Islanders were excluded from the business, and the permits were concentrated into the hands of a favored few. The lawsuit is framed as a challenge to an arbitrary, excessive, and oppressive regulatory policy in violation of substantive and procedural due process.

These three cases all present basic issues of economic liberty, with plaintiffs fighting to earn their share of the American Dream. The broadly applicable precedent of *Brown* v. *Barry* can provide a foundation for subsequent cases advancing economic liberty as a civil right, with each new case building upon the last.

Equality under Law Cases

In *Crawford* v. *Honig*,[8] the Foundation represents several black schoolchildren and their parents in a challenge to a California state rule that prohibits to blacks access to publicly provided I.Q. tests. The rule was crafted following earlier litigation prosecuted by the NAACP to enjoin the use of I.Q. tests for placement of blacks in special education classes. But the state's rule went further, banning I.Q. tests for blacks in most circumstances but making them readily available to whites, Hispanics, and Asians. In tones reminiscent of *Plessy*, school authorities informed the named plaintiff's mother that Crawford, who is half Hispanic, could take the test if she reclassified him as Hispanic.

The lawsuit takes no position on the usefulness of I.Q. tests, but argues the simple equal protection principle that if such tests are available to some, they may not be precluded to others on the basis of race. The case also confronts the NAACP's paternalistic approach toward its constituency, arguing instead for the opportunity of all individuals to control their own destinies free from patronizing race-based assumptions.

In *Jenkins* v. *State of Missouri*,[9] the Foundation represents several black schoolchildren and their parents in a challenge to the Kansas City school district's racial quota for admissions to magnet schools. The schools, created under an ongoing desegregation order, are designed to provide high-quality educational opportunities. But in order to promote racial balance, the district "capped" attendance of black students in a set proportion to whites. As a result, seats in these schools are held empty since the school district deems the number of white students inadequate. The lawsuit thus goes to the core of whether the objective of a school desegregation suit is equal educational opportunities or racial balance.

In *Stone* v. *Board of Education of Prince George's County*,[10] the Center for Civil Rights represents public school teachers, white and black, in a challenge to a school board's racial quota policy for teacher assignments. Each year, the district involuntarily transfers teachers to maintain racial balance in each school's faculty. Although the school district is under continuing desegregation orders, the district court found in 1983 that the district never has discriminated in teacher assignments. The lawsuit thus deals both with the limits of desegregation and the authority of public entities to classify and discriminate on the basis of race.

All three cases present instances of racial classifications harming their intended beneficiaries. Sadly, such instances are no longer rare, and these cases underscore the dangers inherent in any departure from the principle of equality under law.

These cases all possess a number of common characteristics. Each is a federal court action raising major issues of constitutional law. Each involves sympathetic plaintiffs fighting the heavy hand of government oppression. Each reflects an attempt to move the law forward in a systematic, step-by-step quest to regain protection for some of our most fundamental individual rights. Many more cases like them may be necessary before the battle is won.

ENDNOTES

1. *Brown* v. *Barry*, 710 F. Supp. 352 (D.D.C. 1989).
2. *Brown* v. *Barry*, No. 88–0565, slip op. at 5–8 (D.D.C. 14 Oct. 1988).
3. *Id.*, p. 7.
4. *Brown* v. *Barry*, 710 F. Supp. at 355.
5. *Id.*, p. 356 (citation omitted).
6. No. 89–1245 (S.D. Tex., filed 11 Apr. 1989).
7. No. 89–2269 (D.D.C., filed 14 Aug. 1989).
8. No. C–89–0014–RFP (N.D. Cal., filed 20 May 1988).
9. No. 77–0420–CV–W–4 (D. Mo.), motion to modify on behalf of Ronika Newton et al., filed 13 July 1989.
10. No. K–89–289 (D. Md., filed 1988).

INDEX

Abram, Morris, 16, 32, 39, 105
Absolute rights, 17–8
Access to foreign commerce, right of, 62
Access to navigable waters in U.S., right of, 62
Adams, John, 19
Adams, Samuel, 21
adverse impact, 106, 114–22, 126
affirmative action, 5, 38, 112, 112n
Aladdin's Castle, Inc. v. *City of Mesquite*, 84
Allen, William B., 104
Allick v. *Lujan*, 147
Allott, Gordon, 104
Althusius, 16
Amaya, Mary, 93–4, 128n.3
Anti-Jitney Law of 1924, 48, 146
Antitrust, 81, 85
Assembly, right of freedom of, 62
Atonio. See Wards Cove Packing Co. v. *Atonio*
Avins, Alfred, 50, 69

Bakke (*Regents of the University of California* v. *Bakke*), 107, 109

Barnett, Randy E., 23, 78
Barry, Marion, 11
Bartlett, Steve, 5
Belz, Herman, 26, 51, 56, 63–4
Berea College v. *Kentucky*, 101, 128n.25
Berry, Mary Frances, 102
Bill of Rights. *See under* Constitution, U.S.
Bingham, John A., 56–7, 59
Black Codes, 25, 54–5, 69–70
Blackmun, Harry, 108–9, 117
Black separatist movement, 31
Blackstone, Sir William, 19, 23
    civil liberty, 50
    fundamental rights, 20
    natural rights, 17–8, 26–7, 59
Bolling v. *Sharpe*, 96n
Boreman, Arthur, 57, 58
Bork, Robert H., 60n
Bradley, Joseph P., 58, 61, 66–67
Brennan, William, 108, 109, 126
Brown, Ego, 11–3, 14, 18, 40, 49, 127, 137, 143, 144–5. *See also Brown* v. *Barry*
Brown, Henry B., 99–100
Brown v. *Barry*, 11–3, 84–5, 145–7

Brown v. *Board of Education*, 78, 102–6, 126
  busing, 14
  educational opportunity, equal, 122
  empowerment, 6
  natural rights, 30
  separate but equal doctrine assailed, 6, 29, 30
Burgess, John W., 68
Busing, 3, 33, 37, 104, 123–5. *See also Brown* v. *Board of Education*; Educational opportunity, equal
Butler, Benjamin F., 97
Butler, Stuart, 4–5

Carpenter, Matthew H., 60
Cavazos, Lauro, 5
Chambers, Julius L., 126
Changing Course: Civil Rights at the Crossroads (C. Bolick), 1, 2, 74n
Chase, Salmon P., 61
Chavez, Cesar, 47
Citizenship
  judicial decisions: *Dred Scott* v. *Sandford*, 62; *Slaughter-House Cases*, 63–5, 66
  national, 85. *See also* States rights
City of Cleburne v. *Cleburne Living Center*, 82–3, 84–5, 126–7
City of New Orleans v. *Dukes*, 73, 79
City of Richmond v. *J. A. Croson Co.*, 109–12, 112n
Civil law, 3
Civil liberty, 18, 27
Civil Rights Act of 1866, 26, 27, 53, 55–7, 65, 66
Civil Rights Act of 1875, 69
Civil Rights Act of 1964, 3, 5–6, 29, 30, 104–5, 114. *See also* Title VII
Civil rights, definition of, 14–5, 19–20, 27, 51
Civil War, 3, 16, 54. *See also* Reconstruction era
Clark, Thomas, 105
Cleburne. See City of Cleburne v. *Cleburne Living Center*
Colorblindness
  Civil Rights Act of 1964, 105
  Constitution, U.S., 102, 103, 105, 109
  society, 4, 29

Commentaries (W. Blackstone), 17
Commerce, interstate, 81
Commission on Civil Rights, U.S., 102
Committee on the Status of Black Americans, 38
Common law, 17, 59, 66, 67
Common Sense (T. Paine), 19
Competition, right to, 61
Congress of Racial Equality, 29
Congress, U.S., 57, 68. *See also* Reconstruction-era legislation
  quotas, 115, 120
  Reconstruction era, 26, 27, 56–7, 68
  Republicans: civil rights initiatives, 69; post–Civil War, 25; reactions to *Slaughter-House Cases* decision, 68–9
Constitution, U.S., 16, 18, 22, 26, 72–3, 96, 100. *See also* Due process; Equal protection; Privileges or immunities clause; Takings clause
  amendments, Civil War–era, 3, 61, 67. *See also* Reconstruction–era legislation
  Bill of Rights, 16, 23, 26, 35, 53, 58, 85
  Fifth Amendment, 96n
  Ninth Amendment, 18, 23
  Tenth Amendment, 23
  Thirteenth Amendment, 25, 27, 54, 61
  Fourteenth Amendment. *See* Fourteenth Amendment
  Fifteenth Amendment, 25
  Twenty-Fourth Amendment, 30
Contract, freedom to, 50, 51, 52, 55, 96n
  judicial decisions: *Lochner* v. *New York*, 70; *Slaughter-House Cases*, 63–4, 78; *West Coast Hotel Co.* v. *Parrish*, 72–3
Corfield v. *Coryell*, 57, 59, 62, 66, 67
Corwin, Edward, 61
Court of Appeals
  Fifth Circuit, 84, 124
  Ninth Circuit, 84, 119
  Tenth Circuit, 124
Crawford, Desmond. *See Crawford* v. *Honig*
Crawford v. *Honig*, 93–5, 128n.3, 147–8
Crime, 112n
Croson. See City of Richmond v. *A. Croson Co.*
Curtis, Michael Kent, 27, 61, 64

Davis–Bacon Act, 70, 127
Declaration of Independence, 16
    economic liberty, 67
    equality under law, 2, 24, 93, 97
    equal protection, 96n
    natural rights, 21, 27, 29–30, 59
DeFunis, Marco, 35, 110. *See also DeFunis
    v. Odegaard*
DeFunis v. *Odegaard*, 107
Democrats. *See under* Congress, U.S.
Desegregation. *See* Educational
    opportunity, equal
Detlefsen, Robert, 16
de Tocqueville, Alexis, 21–2
Discrimination, 38, 50, 75, 104, 116, 124,
    141, 148. *See also Crawford* v. *Honig*;
    Quotas
    poverty, 126
    reverse, 4, 37, 107, 137
Dorn, James, 50, 71–2
Dorsey, Stuart, 75
Douglas, William O., 107, 113
Douglass, Frederick, 3, 24
Dowell. *See Oklahoma City Board of
    Education* v. *Dowell*
Dred Scott v. *Sandford*, 62, 69
DuBois, W.E.B., 28, 106
Due process, 96, 96n, 147
    judicial decisions: *Lochner* v. *New York*,
        70–2; *Moore* v. *City of East
        Cleveland*, 83–4; *Sinaloa Lake
        Owners Ass'n* v. *City of Simi
        Valley*, 84; *Slaughter-House Cases*,
        60, 80, 81
    substantive due process, 52, 70, 71–2, 76,
        84, 147
Dukes, Nancy, 73–4. *See also City of New
    Orleans* v. *Dukes*
Dworkin, Ronald, 34–5

Eaton, William, 52
Economic liberty, 52, 53–86. *See also Brown*
    v. *Barry*; *Brown* v. *Board of Education*;
    Jim Crow laws; *Plessy* v. *Ferguson*;
    Santos, Alfredo
    Constitutional guarantee, 52, 144–5
    Declaration of Independence, 67
    government, role of, 75–6, 120

impaired, 53–4, 74
    litigation strategy, 127, 143
    privileges or immunities, 79, 81, 85
    Supreme Court, U.S., 70–1, 98; *City of
        New Orleans* v. *Dukes*, 73–4; *City
        of Cleburne* v. *Cleburne Living
        Center*, 82–3; *Lochner* v. *New
        York*, 70–1; *Slaughter-House Cases*,
        7–8, 64, 67, 68–9, 78, 80n; *Yick Wo*
        v. *Hopkins*, 70
Economic status. *See* Discrimination:
    poverty
Educational opportunity, equal, 38, 40,
    41n.5, 49, 122–5. *See also* Busing;
    Nevels, Mark Anthony; Separate
    but equal
    judicial decisions, *Crawford* v. *Honig*,
        93–5. *See also* Bakke; *Brown* v.
        Board of Education; *Plessy* v.
        Ferguson
    judicial remedies, 6, 124–5
    legislative initiatives, 68–9
    litigation strategies, 124–6, 143, 147
    NAACP program, 29
    quotas, 7, 13, 35, 36, 48, 112, 112n
    racial balance, 36, 104, 106, 122–3
    voucher remedy, 125
EEOC. *See* Equal Employment
    Opportunity Commission, U.S.
Employment opportunity, equal, 29, 48, 49,
    59. *See also Slaughter-House Cases*
    empowerment right, 48
    labor shortages, 38
    government restrictions, 49
Empowerment, 4–6, 39, 48, 136–8
    Crawford v. *Honig*, 94
    economic liberty, 76
    educational opportunity, 125
    equal protection, 127
    property rights, 50
    strategies for, 5–6, 8
Enforcement, civil rights measures, 136–7
Entitlements, group, 15, 32–3, 36–7, 39,
    98, 137
    ineffective strategy, 6, 37–9
Entrepreneurship, 12, 112n, 145, 146–7. *See
    also* Brown, Ego; *Brown* v. *Barry*; *City
    of New Orleans* v. *Dukes*; Santos,
    Alfredo
Equal Employment Advisory Council, 117
Equal Employment Opportunity

Commission, U.S., 13, 106–7, 114, 116, 121
Equal opportunity, 15, 112, 112n
    revisionist view, 33–5, 39
Equal protection, 82, 96, 96n, 97–101, 125–7
    judicial decisions, 84–5, 98–9, 127;
        Bakke, 107–8, 109; *Bolling* v.
        Sharpe, 96n; *Brown* v. *Board of
        Education*, 103; *City of Richmond
        v. J. A. Croson Co.*, 110–2; *Moore
        v. City of East Cleveland*, 83; *San
        Antonio* v. *Rodriguez*, 126;
        Slaughter-House Cases, 61, 80, 81;
        Yick Wo v. *Hopkins*, 70. See also
        Berea College v. *Kentucky*;
        Discrimination: poverty; *Kotch* v.
        *Bd. of River Port Com'rs for Port
        of New Orleans*; *Plessy* v. *Ferguson*
    voucher remedy, 125
Equal treatment, 32, 35–6, 100
Equality of outcomes, 20, 31, 126.
    See also Busing; Discrimination;
        Educational opportunity, equal;
        Quotas; Set–asides
    Fourteenth Amendment, 97, 98
    ineffective strategy, 37–8, 39–40
    1960s legislation, 32, 105
    revisionist agenda, 15, 33–9
Equality of results. See Equality
    of outcomes
Equality of rights, 6, 27, 34, 50
    Paine, Thomas, 20, 93
    revisionist view, 33, 35–6
Equality under law, 2, 7, 31, 95–8, 99–127,
    137. See also Equal protection
    Fourteenth Amendment, 27
    Supreme Court, U.S., 106; *Brown* v.
        Board of Education, 29, 103, 105;
        Crawford v. *Honig*, 94–5; *DeFunis
        v. Odegaard*, 107; *Korematsu* v.
        United States, 101–2; *Slaughter-
        House Cases*, 76
    litigation strategies, 7, 103–6, 107, 112–4,
        121–2, 124–8, 146–8
    revisionist agenda, 30
Executive Order 11246, 114, 121

Farmer, James, 29
Federalist No. 10 (J. Madison), 22, 95
Field, Stephen, 47, 61, 64–5, 66

Firefighters Local Union No. 1784 v. *Stotts*,
    109
First principles, 2, 3, 9
Foner, Eric, 19
Fourteenth Amendment, 25, 27, 53, 60, 61,
    63–4. See also Equal protection;
        Natural rights; Privileges or
        immunities
    economic liberty, 54–60, 70–1, 73, 76,
        145–7
    empowerment, 6
    judicial decisions: *DeFunis* v. *Odegaard*,
        107; *Lochner* v. *New York*, 70,
        76–7. See also *Plessy* v. *Ferguson*;
        Slaughter-House Cases
    litigation strategy, 6–8, 121n
    quotas, 121n
    racial classification, 109, 110
Franklin, Benjamin, 24
Freedom of assembly, right of, 62
Frelinghuysen, Frederick, 58
Fried, Charles, 25, 77
Fullilove v. *Klutznick*, 109
Fundamental rights, 2, 6, 7, 20, 27, 30, 98,
    136, 149

Garrison, William Lloyd, 3, 24, 28, 40, 54
Gierke, Otto, 16–7
Glazer, Nathan, 4, 39–40, 105, 123
Gold, Michael, 117
Goldstein, Barry, 11
Government, role of, 20–31, 33, 118
    business regulation, 74–6, 78, 145–7
    civil liberty, 18, 27
    equality, principles of, 7, 49, 51, 54–60,
        81–6, 95–9, 145–7
    judicial decisions: *Cleburne*, 127;
        Slaughter-House Cases, 67; *Yick
        Wo* v. *Hopkins*, 70
    privileges or immunities, 77, 78
    quotas, 114
    racial classifications, 99, 102, 106
    states rights, 60, 68
Griggs v. *Duke Power Co.*, 114–7
Grotius, 16
Group. See Entitlements, group
Gudridge, Patrick, 76–7

Habeus corpus, right of, 62

Hamilton, Alexander, 23, 24
Hamilton, William T., 59
Harlan, John M., 83, 100–1, 103, 104,
    109, 113
Harrington, Michael, 33
Hayek, Friedrich, 36, 51
Heritage Foundation, 4
Higginbotham, Patrick, 124
Hobbes, Thomas, 16
Holmes, Oliver Wendell, 25, 71–2, 77
Hooks, Benjamin, 102
Housing, 4, 33, 113
Howard, Jacob, 58, 97
Hughes, Charles Evans, 72
Humphrey, Hubert H., 29, 104

Individual rights, 15, 59–60, 136–7, 148
International Brotherhood of Teamsters v.
    United States, 116

Jackson, Jesse, 33
Jackson, Robert, 101–2, 106, 113
Jay, John, 24
Jefferson, Thomas, 15, 29
Jenkins v. *State of Missouri*, 148
Jennings, Peter, 11
Jim Crow laws, 12, 13–4, 48n, 69–70, 74,
    145–6
Johnson, Andrew, 56
Johnson v. *Transportation Agency*, 109, 110
Judicial standards, 77, 117, 120, 121. *See
    also* Due process: substantive;
    Rational basis; Reasonableness
    test; Strict scrutiny
Judiciary, 28, 48, 51–2, 59, 136. *See also*
    Supreme Court, U.S.

Karlin, Norman, 73, 76
Kemp, Jack, 5
Kennedy, Anthony, 111
Kent, James, 17, 26, 59
King, Martin Luther, Jr., 39
    first principles, 2, 3
    "I have a dream" speech, 9, 29–30, 105
    natural rights, 15
Korematsu v. *United States*, 101–2
Kotch v. *Bd. of River Port Com'rs for Port
    of New Orleans*, 82

Kozinski, Alex, 84
Kuchel, Thomas, 104–5
Kurland, Philip, 76, 77–8

Labor, 49, 51, 55, 66, 70
laissez-faire, 54
Landmark Legal Foundation, 41n.5, 128n.3,
    Center for Civil Rights, 8, 145–9
Lawrence, William, 26, 55–6
Lawyer's Committee for Civil Rights, 12–3
Levy, Leonard, 73–4, 75–6
Lewis, John, 39
Lincoln, Abraham, 24, 106
Litigation strategies, 1, 6–8, 112–3, 121–2,
    123–7, 135–8, 139–43, 145–9
    amicus curiae, 140, 142
    Federal courts, 140–1, 149
    guidelines for success, 139–43
    public opinion, 8, 142, 146
    skills required, 139
    summary judgment, 142, 146, 147
    systematic strategy development, 79–85,
        141, 149
Local 28, Sheet Metal Workers v. *EEOC*,
    109
Lochner, Louis, 52. *See also Lochner* v.
    New York
Lochner v. *New York*, 52, 52n, 70, 72,
    76, 79
Locke, John, 17, 19, 20, 29
Lofgren, Charles A., 61, 99, 101, 103

Macey, Jonathan, 95–6
Madison, James, 22, 51, 73, 95
Magna Carta (Charta), 26, 68, 85, 136
Maltz, Earl M., 114, 119
Marshall, Thurgood, 85, 105–6, 109,
    126, 143
    Brown v. *Board of Education*, 29,
        102–4, 143
Martin v. *Wilks*, 112, 125
Meredith, James, 143
Miller, Samuel F., 61, 62
Milliken v. *Bradley*, 124
Moore v. *City of East Cleveland*, 83
Movement, freedom of, 62
Murray, Charles, 48–9, 122

NAACP, 6, 9, 28–9, 86, 126, 147–8
  judicial decisions: *Brown* v. *Board of*
    Education, 102, 103n; *Crawford* v.
    Honig, 93–5; *Plessy* v. *Ferguson*,
    76, 102–4; *Slaughter-House Cases*,
    76
  Legal Defense and Educational Fund,
    11, 13, 126, 140
  separate but equal, 6, 126, 135
National Association for the
  Advancement of Colored
  People. *See* NAACP
National Center for Neighborhood
  Enterprise, 5
National Park Service, U.S., 147
Natural law. *See* Natural rights
Natural rights, 2, 8, 15–28, 53, 59. *See*
  also Brown v. *Board of Education*;
  Declaration of Independence
  Constitution, U.S., embodied in, 18, 26,
    50–1, 53, 96–7
  departures from, 30–31, 40
  natural law, 2, 16, 40
  1960s legislation, 30
  Paine, Thomas, 2, 15–6
  Supreme Court, U.S., 98; *Slaughter-*
    House Cases, 63–4, 78
Nevels, Mark Anthony, 13–4, 40, 107, 123,
  137
Newblatt, Stewart, 108–9
Nollan v. *California Coastal Comm'n*, 140n
Norton, Eleanor Holmes, 106–7, 114

O'Connor, Sandra Day, 109–10, 111
Oklahoma City Board of Education v.
  Dowell, 123
Other America, The (M. Harrington), 33
Otis, James, 22

Pacific Legal Foundation, 140n
Paine, Thomas, 1–3, 9, 19–21, 24, 26, 35
  equality under law, 95, 101, 106
  equal rights, 96
  first principles, 2–4
  natural rights, 2, 15–6
Peckham, Rufus, 70
Plessy, Homer Adolph, 94, 99. *See also*
  Plessy v. *Ferguson*
Plessy v. *Ferguson*, 7–8, 28, 69, 76, 137.

  See also Brown v. *Board of Education*
  civil rights, set-backs to, 86, 99–102,
    105, 122, 126
  efforts to overturn, 81, 127
Police power, 64, 67, 70–71
Powell, Lewis F., 83, 107–8, 109
Pratt, John H., 85
Privileges or immunities clause, 6–7, 56–9,
  61, 63–4, 85–6, 96. *See also under*
  Economic liberty
  Civil Rights Act of 1875, 69
  government regulation, 78, 96n
  litigation strategy, 76–9, 84
  Slaughter-House Cases, 7–8, 60, 60n,
    64–5, 78
Property rights, 49, 51, 51n, 55, 84, 98
  Constitution, U.S., protects, 22, 76–7
  empowerment, 48, 50
  judicial decisions: *Lochner* v. *New York*,
    71; *Slaughter-House Cases*, 67, 78
  limits on, 34, 37
  natural rights, 18, 52
Public accommodations, 69
Public transportation. *See* Transportation
Pursuit of happiness, 22, 66. *See also*
  Declaration of Independence

Quotas, 33, 37, 38. *See also* Title VII
  adverse impact, 114–22
  Civil Rights Act of 1964, 105
  educational, 7, 13–4, 35, 36, 49, 107–8,
    112n, 113, 147–8
  employment, 7, 75, 110, 147
  judicial decisions: *Bakke*, 107–8, 109;
    Griggs v. *Duke Power Co.*, 114–6
  limits on equality, 102, 109, 112, 113
  litigation strategies, 121, 141

Racial balance, 141. *See also Brown* v.
  Board of Education; Nevels,
  Mark Anthony
  educational, 37, 104, 122–3, 147–8
  employment, 110, 120, 147
  quotas, use of, 3, 113, 147–8. *See also*
    Quotas
Racial classification, 106–29. *See also*
  Nevels, Mark Anthony
  government, 98, 147
  judicial decisions, 103, 107–13. *See also*

Crawford v. *Honig*
  litigation strategies, 112–3, 146–7
Racial discrimination. *See* Discrimination
Racial distinctions, 100–2
Racial neutrality, 4, 70, 111, 112n. *See also*
  Colorblindness
Raspberry, William, 9, 122
Rational basis, 73, 78–9, 81–2, 82–3, 85,
  98, 144–5
Rawls, John, 34
Reasonableness test, 100, 103, 108, 109–10
Reconstruction era, 30, 31, 50, 54–60, 99
  legislation, 25–6, 27–8, 67
Regents of the University of California v.
  Bakke. See Bakke
Religion, freedom of, 125
Republicans. *See under* Congress, U.S.
Revisionist agenda, civil rights, 31–40, 118–9
Revolutionary era, American, 16, 29–30.
  See also Declaration of Independence
Rivarde v. *School Dist. of Kansas City*, 125,
  134n, 143
Roosevelt, Franklin D., 52
Rousseau, Jean Jacques, 16
Rustin, Bayard, 32

San Antonio v. *Rodriguez*, 126
Santos, Alfredo, 47–8, 49, 74, 86, 127, 137,
  145–6
Santos v. *City of Houston*, 145–6. *See also*
  Santos, Alfredo
Scalia, Antonin, 47, 110–3, 112n, 113
Schurz, Carl, 55
Separate but equal, 6, 30, 69, 86, 99,
  103, 126
Set–asides, 3, 33, 37, 48, 109, 112
Sherman Antitrust Act, 80, 85
Sherman, John, 59
Siegan, Bernard, 26, 52
Sinaloa Lake Owners Ass'n v. *City of Simi
  Valley*, 84
Slaughter-House Cases, 28, 60–9, 75–86
  aftermath, 68–86
  economic liberty, 7–8, 66, 68, 69, 70
  legislative strategy, 78, 80–1
  police power, 64, 67
  privileges or immunities, 7–8, 60, 61–2
  rights involved in, 62, 67, 68
  Supreme Court, U.S., decisions, 62–9
Slavery, 24, 26, 33, 48n, 56, 62

abolition, 5, 18, 24, 25, 30, 31, 40, 54
  antithesis of liberty, 24, 54
  antithesis of equality, 96
Social Statics (H. Spencer), 25, 26
Souls of Black Folk, The (W. DuBois), 28
Spangler v. *Pasadena City Board of
  Education*, 124
Spencer, Herbert, 25, 26, 54
Spinoza, Baruch, 16
States rights, 58–9, 63, 64, 66–7, 68, 69, 96
Stephens, Alexander, 24
Stevens, John Paul, 97–8, 109
Stevens, Thaddeus, 97
Stone v. *Board of Education of Prince
  George's County*, 148
Strict scrutiny, 98, 109, 111
Substantive due process. *See under*
  Due process
Sumner, Charles, 6
Sunstein, Cass, 96
Supreme Court, U.S., 53, 98–9, 106, 141.
  See also cases listed individually
Sutherland, George, 72
Swayne, Noah H., 61, 66, 67–8

Taking Rights Seriously (R. Dworkin), 34
Takings clause (Constitution, U.S.), 77, 81
Teamsters, International Brotherhood of, 4,
  116
Tempting of America, The (R. Bork), 60n
tenBroek, Jacobus, 60
Tests
  employment, 121
  I.Q., 93–4, 147–8
Thayer, Martin, 55
Theory of Justice, A (J. Rawls), 34
Thomas, Clarence, 118
Title VII, 85, 104. *See also* Civil Rights
  Act of 1964
  employment opportunity, 115
  equal opportunity, 118
  legislative strategy, 80, 81
  quotas, 109, 117, 120, 121, 121n
  racial classification, 109, 115
Transportation, 29, 79, 99
Truly Disadvantaged, The (W. Wilson),
  38–9
Trumbull, Lyman, 27
Tussman, Joseph, 60

United States Employment Service, 122
United States v. *Overton*, 125
United States v. *Paradise*, 109
United Steelworkers v. *Weber*, 109

Village of Arlington Heights
    v. *Metropolitan Housing*
    Development Corp., 121n
Villard, Oswald Garrison, 29
Voting Rights Act of 1965, 30
Voting rights, equal, 28
Voucher remedy, 125

Wards Cove Packing Co. v. *Atonio*, 119–22
Washington, Booker T., 28
Washington, Bushrod, 57, 62, 66
Welfare, 33, 37, 48–9, 75, 112n
West Coast Hotel Co. v. *Parrish*, 72
White, Byron, 119
Williams, Harrison, 105
Williams, Walter, 74
Wilson, Henry, 27, 93, 97
Wilson, James F., 97
Wilson, William Julius, 38–9
Woodson, Robert, 5
Wygant v. *Jackson Board of Education*,
    109, 111–2

Yick Wo v. *Hopkins*, 70
Young, Whitney, 33

ABOUT THE AUTHOR

Clint Bolick is director of the Landmark Legal Foundation Center for Civil Rights in Washington, D.C. Bolick is the architect of a litigation program emphasizing economic liberty and other aspects of individual empowerment.

Bolick previously served in both the United States Department of Justice, Civil Rights Division, and the Equal Employment Opportunity Commission. He is author of *Changing Course: Civil Rights at the Crossroads* (Transaction, 1988); and is co-author of the forthcoming *Help Wanted: How Companies Can Survive and Thrive in the Coming Worker Shortage* (McGraw-Hill) and *Grass Roots Tyranny and the Limits of Federalism* (Cato Institute).

The Pacific Research Institute produces studies that explore long-term solutions to difficult issues of public policy. The Institute seeks to facilitate a more active and enlightened discourse on these issues and to broaden understanding of market processes, government policy, and the rule of law. Through the publication of scholarly books and the sponsorship of conferences, the Institute serves as an established resource for ideas in the continuing public policy debate.

Institute books have been adopted for courses at colleges, universities, and graduate schools nationwide. More than 175 distinguished scholars have worked with the Institute to analyze the premises and consequences of existing public policy and to formulate possible solutions to seemingly intractable problems. Prestigious journals and major media regularly review and comment upon Institute work. In addition, the Board of Advisors consists of internationally recognized scholars, including two Nobel laureates.

The Pacific Research Institute is an independent, tax exempt, 501(c)(3) organization and as such is supported solely by the sale of its books and by the contributions from a wide variety of foundations, corporations, and individuals. This diverse funding base and the Institute's refusal to accept government funds enable it to remain independent.

OTHER STUDIES IN PUBLIC POLICY BY
THE PACIFIC RESEARCH INSTITUTE

URBAN TRANSIT
The Private Challenge to Public Transportation
Edited by Charles A. Lave
Foreword by John Meyer

POLITICS, PRICES, AND PETROLEUM
The Political Economy of Energy
By David Glasner
Foreword by Paul W. MacAvoy

RIGHTS AND REGULATION
Ethical, Political, and Economic Issues
Edited by Tibor M. Machan and M. Bruce Johnson
Foreword by Aaron Wildavsky

FUGITIVE INDUSTRY
The Economics and Politics of Deindustrialization
By Richard B. McKenzie
Foreword by Finis Welch

MONEY IN CRISIS
The Federal Reserve, the Economy, and Monetary Reform
Edited by Barry N. Siegel
Foreword by Leland B. Yeager

NATURAL RESOURCES
Bureaucratic Myths and Environmental Management
By Richard Stroup and John Baden
Foreword by William Niskanen

FIREARMS AND VIOLENCE
Issues of Public Policy
Edited by Don B. Kates, Jr.
Foreword by John Kaplan

WATER RIGHTS
Scarce Resource Allocation, Bureaucracy, and the Environment
Edited by Terry L. Anderson
Foreword by Jack Hirshleifer

LOCKING UP THE RANGE
Federal Land Controls and Grazing
By Gary D. Libecap
Foreword by Jonathan R.T. Hughes

THE PUBLIC SCHOOL MONOPOLY
A Critical Analysis of Education and the State in American Society
Edited by Robert B. Everhart
Foreword by Clarence J. Karier

RESOLVING THE HOUSING CRISIS
Government Policy, Demand, Decontrol, and the Public Interest
Edited with an Introduction by M. Bruce Johnson

OFFSHORE LANDS
Oil and Gas Leasing and Conservation on the Outer Continental Shelf
By Walter J. Mead, et al.
Foreword by Stephen L. McDonald

ELECTRIC POWER
Deregulation and the Public Interest
Edited by John C. Moorhouse
Foreword by Harold Demsetz

TAXATION AND THE DEFICIT ECONOMY
Fiscal Policy and Capital Formation in the United States
Edited by Dwight R. Lee
Foreword by Michael J. Boskin

THE AMERICAN FAMILY AND STATE
Edited by Joseph R. Peden and Fred R. Glahe
Foreword by Robert Nisbet

DEALING WITH DRUGS
Consequences of Government Control
Edited by Ronald Hamowy
Foreword by Dr. Alfred Freedman

CRISIS AND LEVIATHAN
Critical Episodes in the Growth of American Government
By Robert Higgs
Foreword by Arthur A. Ekirch, Jr.

THE NEW CHINA
Comparative Economic Development in Mainland China, Taiwan, and Hong Kong
By Alvin Rabushka

ADVERTISING AND THE MARKET PROCESS
A Modern Economic View
By Robert B. Ekelund, Jr. and David S. Saurman
Foreword by Israel M. Kirzner

HEALTH CARE IN AMERICA
The Political Economy of Hospitals and Health Insurance
Edited by H.E. Frech III
Foreword by Richard Zeckhauser

POLITICAL BUSINESS CYCLES
The Political Economy of Money, Inflation, and Unemployment
Edited by Thomas D. Willett
Foreword by Axel Leijonhufvud

WHEN GOVERNMENT GOES PRIVATE
Successful Alternatives to Public Services
By Randall Fitzgerald

THE YELLOWSTONE PRIMER
Land and Resource Management in the Greater Yellowstone Ecosystem
Edited by John A. Baden and Don Leal

TO PROMOTE THE GENERAL WELFARE
Market Processes vs. Political Transfers
By Richard E. Wagner

For further information on the Pacific Research Institute's program and a catalog of publications, please contact:

PACIFIC RESEARCH INSTITUTE FOR PUBLIC POLICY
177 Post Street
San Francisco, CA 94108
(415) 989-0833